THE
NATIONAL
TRUST
FOR
SCOTLAND
Recipe Book

Also published by Chambers

Trustlands: Photographs of the National Trust for Scotland
by Glyn Satterley

The National Trust for Scotland Recipe Book

Both authors are experts in Scottish cookery and enthusiasts for the best of
Scottish food, traditions and hospitality. Jean Stewart produced a cookery
book to celebrate the jubilee of the Forestry Commission and was for
seven years editor of the magazine *Scottish Home and Country*. Muriel
Hume's career involved teaching, talking and demonstrating about food
throughout Scotland. She first met Jean Stewart some years ago when she
was writing a series of articles on food for the magazine.

THE
NATIONAL
TRUST
FOR
SCOTLAND

Recipe Book

Jean Stewart and Muriel Hume

Published in association with
❦ National Trust for Scotland

Chambers

Published 1990 by W & R Chambers Ltd, 43–45 Annandale Street, Edinburgh EH7 4AZ

British Library Cataloguing in Publication Data
Stewart, Jean
   The National Trust for Scotland recipe book.
   1. Food: Scottish dishes–Recipes
   I. Title II. Hume, Muriel
   641.59411

ISBN 0-550-20004-5

Design by Keith Kail

Typeset by Pillans & Wilson Specialist Litho Printers Limited
    Edinburgh

Printed and bound in Great Britain at the Bath Press, Avon

Contents

Preface

THE NATIONAL TRUST FOR SCOTLAND is delighted to be associated with Chambers in the publication of a further book about its work.

Each year the Trust receives over two million visitors to its properties, many of whom stay long enough to enjoy a meal at one of its restaurants or tea-rooms. Not content with safeguarding the buildings, gardens and countryside in its care, the Trust also seeks to perpetuate some of the old and well-tried Scottish recipes that have been handed down over the years and presents its visitors with the best of Scottish fare.

This book of recipes, culled from many sources, including some from the kitchens of Trust properties, shows the quality and variety of Scottish regional fare and will, we hope, serve as a reminder of all that a visit to a Trust property seeks to provide—fine buildings, good company and excellent Scottish food.

Introduction

SCOTLAND is fortunate in the great variety of food to be harvested from its land and from the seas which surge round its shores.

The seas, rivers and lochs offer a wide choice of fish, while the arable land grows good crops of cereals, soft fruits and vegetables. The pasture land gives excellent grazing to the well-bred cattle and sheep. The high hills, heather-clad moors and forests provide food and shelter for many different types of deer and game.

The diet of the Scots people was always frugal and simple, but wholesome. Either because of an adventurous spirit or an impoverished family, the younger sons of the nobility had a tendency to leave their homeland and travel in foreign parts, usually Europe. They, as we do today, sampled food from other lands and when they returned home, brought with them the ideas and sometimes the cooks from these places. From this we learned to prepare food in many different ways. As times passed and trade with Europe and beyond increased, many strange and exotic foods became more readily available and the French, and to a lesser degree Italian, influence began to be seen in the cookery of Scotland.

Grain, especially oats and barley, played such an important part in the diet that students were given a holiday at half-term to enable them to return to their homes to replenish their meal sacks. From this custom we have the term 'Meal Monday'.

Wheat was not a staple grain in Scotland and consequently was expensive, so bread as we know it today was rare. As most households did all their cooking over an open fire, there were no ovens for baking. In cities like Edinburgh, bakers might have a few wheaten loaves for sale, but they were dear and not in great demand. The womenfolk would take their own pies to the baker to be baked; as in earlier days they would probably have taken them to the bakehouse at the monastery or abbey. Some people might buy a ready-made pie from the baker, so 'take-away' food is not a new twentieth-century idea!

Although we grow fruit and vegetables as a market garden industry, the average Scot did not eat many vegetables except as part of another dish such as broth. Raspberries, cranberries, brambles and rowans grew wild in the countryside and every cottage garden had its black and red currants, gooseberry bushes and a patch of rhubarb.

Milk and milk products were important in the diet. Milk, buttermilk and whey were all consumed in large quantities. Cheeses were made from cow's and sheep's milk in both castle and cottage. Today this cottage industry is once again flourishing in many parts of Scotland.

The Scots are famous for their hospitality. It was considered infamous for a man to lock his door against a stranger. As in past generations we still give a warm welcome to visitors from all parts of the world.

Today, the National Trust for Scotland continues this tradition of hospitality, welcoming literally millions of visitors each year to over one hundred properties in its care. At all the larger properties, visitors can enjoy home baking and good Scottish food from recipes handed down by generations of cooks.

Acknowledgments

THE AUTHORS would like to thank the following for their invaluable assistance:

The National Trust for Scotland for supporting the project from conception to publication and Morag Macdonald for her beautiful drawings; the individual guidebooks to the properties produced by The National Trust for Scotland; the anonymous person in Kirriemuir who gave us the information about the 'heckler' and the recipe for Kirriemuir Heckles; Dr Gordon Burgess, who kindly parted with the recipe for his Granny's Christmas Pudding; Mrs Andrew Gibb who many years ago gave us the recipe for Dubton Pie; Mrs Margaret Horne of the But 'n Ben restaurant in Auchmithie who gave us her recipe for Partan Bree; Mrs Shirley Mathieson who allowed us to use her own special Smokie Mousse recipe; Mrs Margaret Ruxton who handed on the recipe for Oat Crunchies; Anne Drysdale who gave us both Cream of Mustard and Fencible Soup; Stella Roberts, editor of *Scottish Home and Country*; Mrs Jean Philips, now Mrs Stubbs, who gave us the information about the Hurl Pot salmon pool on the river near House of Dun; Marion Hampton who gave us the recipe for Cortachy Trifle; the staff of Arbroath Library for their help in obtaining books for reference.

Bibliography

Black, Maggie, *A Heritage of British Cooking,* Letts, London, 1977

Brown, Catherine, *Catherine Brown's Scottish Cookery,* Richard Drew, Glasgow, 1985

FitzGibbon, Theodora, *A Taste of Scotland,* J. M. Dent, London, 1970

Gillon, Jack, *Chambers Scottish Food Book,* Chambers, Edinburgh, 1989

Grigson, Jane, *The Observer Guide to British Cookery,* Michael Joseph, London, 1984

Hay, George, *A History of Arbroath,* Thomas Buncle, Arbroath, 1899

Hope, Annette, *A Caledonian Feast,* Mainstream, Edinburgh, 1987

King, Aileen and Dunnett, Fiona *Home Book of Scottish Cookery,* Faber & Faber, London, 1973

Lochhead, Marion, *The Scots Household in the Eighteenth Century,* Moray Press, Edinburgh, 1948

Mabey, David and Mabey, Richard *In Search of Food,* Macdonald and Jane's, London, 1978

McNeill, F. Marian, *The Scots Kitchen,* Blackie, London, 1929

Plant, Marjorie, *Domestic Life of Scotland in the Eighteenth Century,* Edinburgh University Press, Edinburgh, 1952

Price Jones, Iris, *Celtic Cookery,* C. Davies, Swansea, 1979

Warren, Janet, *A Feast of Scotland,* Hodder & Stoughton, London, 1979

SOUP POT

She looketh well to the ways of her household, and eateth not the bread of idleness.

PROVERBS

SCOTTISH housewives have always known how to make excellent nourishing soups. Every bit of the animal is used by the frugal cook. Into the pot go beef, mutton or chicken bones, any vegetables that are available, herbs, almonds, indeed 'a'thing'. Red wine or a spoonful of redcurrant jelly may be added to a mutton-based soup, which is delicious accompanied by an oatmeal bannock or barley scone.

A strong stock is the basis of any good soup. Get the butcher to chop up the large bones so that the marrow escapes in the cooking. To make really brown stock, put the bones in a hot oven to brown. Leaving the skins on onions gives good colour to stock. Serve crisp croûtons with a creamy soup to enhance the appearance as well as the taste.

Soup was a staple part of the agricultural workers' diet and in the Angus Folk Museum at Glamis you can see a fascinating selection of stock pots, pans, bowls, sieves and other cooking utensils collected from the neighbourhood.

After-a-Day-in-the-Open-Air Soup

Quickly made, and very warming, this soup is just the thing for supper after a day's outdoor activity. It is also very useful for using up the extra uneaten toast from breakfast!

Serves 6–8

4 large onions	salt and pepper
25 g (1 oz) butter	3 slices of brown bread, toasted
1.25 litres (2 pints) beef stock	grated Cheddar cheese

PEEL and slice the onions and brown very well in the butter in a large pan. Add the stock and seasoning. Bring to the boil. Float the brown bread toast in the stock and simmer for 30 minutes. Cool, then liquidize. Reheat when required and serve with a bowl of grated cheese.

Apple and Watercress Soup

This mixture of flavours and colours is light and summery, looks delicate and tastes delicious.

Serves 6–8

2 15 ml spoons (2 tablespoons) butter	150 ml (¼ pint) double cream (or top of the milk)
1 Spanish onion, peeled and sliced	2 egg yolks
1 large bunch watercress	2 eating apples
600 ml (1 pint) chicken stock	juice of ½ lemon
1 5 ml spoon (1 teaspoon) curry powder	salt and pepper
1 15 ml spoon (1 tablespoon) cornflour	watercress leaves, to garnish

MELT the butter in a pan, add the onion and cook gently until soft but not brown. Stir in the watercress and chicken stock. Add the cornflour and curry powder mixed with a little water to make a thin paste, bring to the boil and simmer for 8 minutes. Heat the cream gently in a pan, then add the egg yolks and stir gradually into the soup. Remove from the heat and liquidize, along with 1 apple, peeled, cored and sliced. Season to taste and chill. Peel the remaining apple, dice it and leave in lemon juice. When ready to serve the soup, stir in the diced apple and garnish with watercress leaves.

Cream of Mustard Soup

Mustard is thought to have come from the Norsemen who traded with the east coast and settled in some areas of the north. In the Isle of Arran mustard seeds are grown especially for the manufacture of the famous whole grain Arran mustard. Its crunchy texture is a good contrast to the smooth English and French mustards made with mustard powder.

Serves 6–8

1 bunch spring onions
25 g (1 oz) butter
1 15 ml spoon (1 tablespoon) mustard powder
1 15 ml spoon (1 tablespoon) plain flour
600 ml (1 pint) vegetable or chicken stock

2 15 ml spoons (2 tablespoons) French mustard
2.5 ml (½ teaspoon) lemon juice
2 egg yolks
300 ml (½ pint) single cream

FINELY slice the spring onions and reserve about 4 15 ml spoons (4 tablespoons) of the green tops for garnish. Melt the butter and sauté the remaining spring onions. Stir in the powdered mustard and plain flour and cook, stirring, for 1 minute. Stir in the stock, the French mustard and lemon juice and simmer for 5 minutes. Beat the egg yolks and single cream together and stir into the soup over a gentle heat. Cook, stirring all the time until thickened. Do not allow to boil or the soup will curdle. Serve sprinkled with the reserved spring onions.

Culzean Castle

FOR ALMOST 600 YEARS the coastland bordering the Firth of Clyde was dominated by the cliff-top castles and keeps of the Kennedy family, giving them power and protection. When the tumult and feuding of the seventeenth century was over, the influence of the 'improving lairds' began to be felt throughout Scotland. New beginnings in every aspect of Scottish life were taking place and it was the ninth Earl who instigated much of the 'improving' at Culzean.

However, it was his brother, the tenth Earl of Cassillis who commissioned Robert Adam to draw up designs for the rehabilitation of the medieval building of Culzean, the first of which is dated 1777. Adam had absorbed many different attitudes and influences during his travels abroad. At Culzean he set out to show that comfort and strength in a castle were not incompatible, in a way that blended eighteenth-century elegance with sturdy Scottish style and all of it set against a superb background of hill and sea.

In 1969, under the ownership of the National Trust for Scotland and in partnership with the district and regional authorities, Scotland's first Country Park was established at Culzean. Now, over two decades later, many thousands of people of all ages go there each year for recreation and enjoyment. A particular objective is to provide special facilities for children to learn to appreciate and care for their countryside. The Country Park is open all year round and has a broad scope for every kind of activity and event to cater for all tastes. Culzean Castle and Country Park is a community in itself and no effort is spared to administer the estate as such.

A remarkable and imaginative gesture was to make a gift for his lifetime to General Dwight Eisenhower, Supreme Commander of the Allied Forces in Europe and later President of the United States, of a flat in Culzean Castle as a mark of gratitude from the Scottish people. Following the President's death, the flat became the National Guest Flat and is now available for national, business or private hospitality.

(Location: Off A77, 12 m S of Ayr, Strathclyde Region.)

Fencible Soup

*When the threat of invasion by Napoleon was at its height in the first years
of the nineteenth century, the twelfth Earl of Cassillis raised the West
Lowland Fencible Regiment, from which this tasty soup takes its name.*

Serves 6–8

1 medium onion	600 ml (1 pint) stock
25 g (1 oz) butter	milk
1 medium turnip	salt and pepper
3 chillies, fresh or dried, soaked in sherry	a pinch of nutmeg

CHOP the onion and soften in the butter. Peel and cut up the turnip and add to
the onion. Drain the chillies, reserving the liquid, and add to the pan with the
stock. Bring to the boil and simmer until the turnip is soft. Take out the
chillies. Liquidize, adding a little milk if the mixture is too thick. Return to
the pan and add enough milk to give a creamy consistency. Season and add
grated nutmeg. If the soup is not hot enough, add some piquante sherry.
Reheat and let the soup stand for as long as possible, so that the turnip infuses
into the milk. This soup may be made two days in advance. Make sure there
are no chillies in it before serving!

Note: Fresh hot chillies may not be easily come by. Dried chillies soaked in
sherry may be kept for some time; the sherry becomes piquante and may be
used as flavouring for many dishes.

Leek and Potato Soup

*This is the Scots version of the famous French soup known as Vichyssoise.
It can be eaten hot with oatcakes or chilled for a summer lunch.*

Serves 6–8

2 large leeks	2 large potatoes, peeled
1 onion	300 ml (½ pint) milk or cream
50 g (2 oz) butter	chives, chopped, and croûtons,
600 ml (1 pint) chicken stock	to garnish

CHOP the leeks and onion fairly finely and put them with the butter in a pan.
Cover and simmer gently for about 5 minutes without browning. Add the
chicken stock and the potatoes, roughly chopped into pieces. Simmer until
the potatoes are cooked. Put through a fine sieve or liquidize, then return to
the pan. Add the milk or cream, heat but do not allow to boil. Serve with
chives and croûtons.

Hill of Tarvit

IT IS SOMETIMES forgotten nowadays that Scotland was the hub of industrial success and enterprise in the world of the late nineteenth century and the first half of the twentieth century. Ships, railways and many more manufactured products were made in Scotland. Successful manufacturers, of course, became men of considerable wealth, and one of these was Frederick Sharp of Broughty Ferry and Dundee. He had trained in London in the complexities of high finance, and on his return to Dundee entered the jute industry.

The basic jute material came from India, and was then mixed with whale oil, readily available from yet another successful Dundee industry, that of whaling.

In 1906 Robert Lorimer (later knighted in 1911), who was to become a leading Scottish architect of the period and whose family lived in nearby Kellie Castle, was commissioned by Frederick Sharp to build a fitting and commodious house near Cupar for his family. At about the same time, Charles Rennie Mackintosh was building a house for the same purpose for the Blackie family on the other side of Scotland at Helensburgh–but how different these designs were.

The house at Hill of Tarvit sits on a gentle south-facing slope exuding an air of comeliness and stability. The gardens there were also designed by Lorimer and still invite one to linger. The house is full of lovely possessions, reflecting the knowledge and taste of a successful Edwardian gentleman. The treasures of the Burrell Collection are more widely known, but the smaller collection at Tarvit is hardly less remarkable and just as rewarding to visit and enjoy. The tea-room provides an additional attraction for visitors and is much appreciated.

(Location: Off A916, 2½ m S of Cupar, Fife.)

Mulligatawny Soup

*The increased trade with the East and with India in particular introduced
Scots to the delights of spicy food and curries. This soup became popular
with the men who were involved in the jute and other industries and the
recipe was brought home and adapted to suit Scots taste.*

Serves 6–8

1 onion
1 carrot
1 small turnip
1 large apple
40 g (1½ oz) butter
1 heaped 15 ml spoon
  (1 tablespoon) flour
1 15 ml spoon (1 tablespoon)
  curry powder

900 ml (1½ pints) mutton stock
salt and pepper
1 heaped 15 ml spoon
  (1 tablespoon) chutney
1 bay leaf
a pinch of thyme
juice of ½ lemon
parsley, chopped, to garnish

PEEL and chop the onion, carrot, turnip and apple quite finely. Melt the butter
in a pan, add the vegetables and apple and fry until brown. Mix the flour with
the curry powder in a little cold stock. Add to the vegetable mixture and cook
for 10 minutes. Add the remainder of the stock, salt and pepper to taste, and
then add the chutney, bay leaf and thyme. Bring to the boil and simmer for 30
minutes. Liquidize, then pour back into the pan and heat until boiling. Add
the lemon juice and serve garnished with the chopped parsley.

Partan Bree

*One of the classic soups of Scotland, this recipe came from a small fishing
village on the east coast. Sometimes rice is used instead of potatoes as
thickener. Partan is the Scots word for crab and bree is the juice or liquor in
which a food has been cooked.*

Serves 6–8

5 medium potatoes
3 medium onions
3½ litres (6 pints) cold water
2 cooked crabs

salt and pepper
1 15 ml spoon (1 tablespoon)
  cream
parsley, chopped, to garnish

PEEL and chop the potatoes and onions roughly and cook in the water until
soft. Pick the white and brown meat from the crabs and add to the soup, then
liquidize. Season to taste. Reheat and serve with a spoonful of cream and
garnish with chopped parsley.

Purée of Green Pea Soup

Although the recipe uses fresh green peas, this soup can be made with frozen peas but the flavour may not be so good. All Scots gardens would have a row or two of peas.

Serves 6–8

600 ml (1 pint) chicken or
   vegetable stock
450 g (1 lb) fresh green peas
sprigs of parsley

sprigs of mint
salt and pepper
65 ml (2½ fl oz) cream
parsley, chopped, to garnish

BRING the stock to the boil and add the shelled peas, together with a few of their pods, and the parsley and mint sprigs. Cook until tender. Liquidize. Season and reheat, adding the cream just before serving, and sprinkle with chopped parsley. A few spring onions may be added to the peas while cooking to give added delicate flavour. To make a thicker, more creamy soup, add a thin white sauce when reheating the soup.

Bannockburn Heritage Centre

ROBERT THE BRUCE, one of the greatest Scottish heroes, was not only a fine battle commander but knew how to surround himself with men of like heroic calibre: Lord James Douglas, Randolph, Keith, and his own brother Edward Bruce. They were all veterans of years of guerrilla fighting and in their struggle to win Scotland, castle after castle was wrested back—all except the castle of Stirling.

Edward II was counselled by his English advisers to make a stand over Stirling, and set forth from England across the Scottish Border at the head of 20 000 well-trained soldiers, experienced archermen, Welsh and Irish, and outnumbering by nearly four to one the Scottish army.

Heavy troops of English cavalry had to negotiate morass and boggy ground at Bannockburn, playing into the hands of the Scottish army, for Bruce had chosen his ground with consummate skill. He had the total confidence of his men. Sir Alexander Seton, arriving at Bruce's council of war, had described the bad situation Edward's army found itself in, and cried, 'Now's the time and now's the hour—and Scotland shall be free.' And on a June day in 1314 Robert the Bruce gained a decisive victory in what was probably the greatest battle which ever took place on Scottish soil.

In the Bannockburn Heritage Centre is to be found a splendid historical exhibition, 'The Kingdom of the Scots', and an exciting audio-visual presentation of the battle.

(Location: Off M80/M9, 2 m S of Stirling, Central Region.)

Scaraben Hare Soup

If you ask the game dealer or butcher to prepare the hare, be sure to tell him it is for soup and ask him to keep the blood. This is most important as it gives the soup its distinctive flavour and rich colour. The soup should be served in one of the old deep Scots soup plates. It is very nourishing and substantial and no other course is required. Sometimes called Bawd (hare) Bree (liquor in which cooked).

Serves 6–8

1 hare, jointed
salt and pepper
100 g (4 oz) butter
225 g (8 oz) lean ham, chopped
2 litres (3½ pints) stock or water
3 onions

12 peppercorns
a pinch of mace
50 g (2 oz) plain flour
300 ml (½ pint) port wine
8 boiled potatoes

COAT the joints of hare in seasoned flour. Melt half the butter in a large pan and add the ham and the hare pieces, and fry all until light brown. Add the stock, the onions with their skins on, the peppercorns and the mace. Simmer for 3 hours, then skim and strain. Separately, melt the rest of the butter and mix in the flour, stirring until smooth. Add this, with seasonings and the pieces of hare, to the stock, along with the port wine. Simmer for 20 minutes. Pour the blood into a bowl and add a little warm soup. Stir well and return to the pan. Do not boil. Serve a fluffy boiled potato in each large warmed soup plate and pour the soup over.

Scotch Broth

When Dr Johnson, on his tour of the Hebrides in 1786 was asked, 'You never ate it [Scotch broth] before?' he replied, 'No, sir, but I don't care how soon I eat it again'. It is indeed one of the great soups of the world. Usually enough is made for two days and it tastes even better the second day.

Serves 6–8

700 g (1½ lb) neck of mutton
1.25 litres (2 pints) water
1 15 ml spoon (1 tablespoon)
  barley
1 small carrot
½ turnip

1 onion
1 strip of celery
1 5 ml spoon (1 teaspoon)
  parsley, finely chopped
salt and pepper

REMOVE all fat from the meat and cut into small pieces. Put the meat into the water along with its bones and a little salt. Bring slowly to the boil, and skim well. Blanch the barley by putting it into cold water and bringing it to the boil. Then drain. Peel and cut the vegetables into small pieces or cubes and add to the broth when it has cooked for 1 hour. Add the barley. Simmer gently for 3 hours. Carefully remove all the bones. Return the soup to the pan, and bring to the boil. Sprinkle in the parsley and season to taste.

Spinach and Turkey Soup

This was a popular soup for using up the leftovers from the Christmas turkey. Scots gardeners had been growing spinach successfully for many years and by the nineteenth century turkeys were being reared in various parts of the country.

Serves 6–8

450 g (1 lb) spinach
50 g (2 oz) butter or margarine
1 onion, chopped
1 potato, peeled and chopped
900 ml (1½ pints) turkey stock
salt and pepper
1 blade of mace

10 ml (2 teaspoons) lemon juice
1 bay leaf
75 g (3 oz) cooked turkey meat,
  finely chopped
150 ml (¼ pint) single or soured
  cream

WASH the spinach thoroughly, discarding any tough stems. Melt the fat in a pan and fry the onion gently until soft but not coloured. Add the spinach and the potato and sauté gently for 2–3 minutes. Add the stock, seasonings, mace, lemon juice and bay leaf, and bring to the boil, cover and simmer gently for 20–25 minutes or until tender. Discard the mace and bay leaf then sieve or liquidize the soup. Return to the pan, adjust the seasonings and add the turkey meat. Simmer for 2–3 minutes, stir in the cream and serve.

FISH KETTLE

Haddies, caller haddies,
Fresh and loupin' in the creel.

OLD EDINBURGH STREET CRY

SCOTLAND has not only a long coastline with many sheltered bays and inlets but also large stretches of fresh water in lochs and rivers. It is therefore only natural that the Scots are great fish eaters.

Before overfishing and pollution became a sad fact of our modern life, fish such as oysters and mussels were common. Vast mussel beds lay at the mouth of the River Forth and Musselburgh is said to have been named after them. Oysters were so plentiful, and consequently so cheap, that cooks added them to all kinds of dishes, while the fashionable meeting places for the intellectuals in Edinburgh were in the oyster cellars of the Old Town.

The sea was also rich in cod, haddock, herring, mackerel and whiting; but as these supplies were seasonal, it was necessary to preserve some in time of plenty for the long winter months of scarcity. This resulted in the Scots becoming skilled in the art of curing and smoking. From these methods, thought to have been introduced by Norse settlers, we continue to produce delicacies such as smoked salmon, kippers, haddock and 'smokies'.

The Trust, through its Little Houses Improvement Scheme, has helped restore the fishing villages of Fife, such as Crail and Pittenweem. There, selected houses have been bought, restored and sold, with safeguards for their future, and the money revolved to undertake yet more work.

13

Glenfinnan

GLENFINNAN HAS a significant place in the history of the Jacobite uprisings. James VII of Scotland and II of England was a Catholic King, so unpopular that in 1688 he was deposed and the crown given to William of Orange, a Protestant Dutchman, who was married to James's eldest daughter, Mary. Louis XIV of France, ever wishing to further the Catholic cause, supported the claim of James's son to the crown of what was a united kingdom after the Treaty of Union of 1707. This man is known in history as the 'Old Pretender' and it was his son, Charles Edward Stuart–Bonnie Prince Charlie, the 'Young Pretender'–who determined to win the throne for the House of Stuart.

With supreme optimism, but none of the promised French army and little naval support, the 'Young Pretender' and a mere seven companions landed at Loch nan Uamh, near Glenfinnan, on 25 July 1745. The clans gathered to support him, and it was a strange army of men whose character was a mixture of absolute obedience to the call of their clan chief and of independence of spirit. This independence allowed the man who perhaps had a crop to sow to set off home whenever he judged the moment was right. This was not seen as desertion, as it would have been in the disciplined Hanoverian troops.

And so the Prince's standard, of red silk with a white spot in the centre, was raised at Glenfinnan beside Loch Shiel on 19 August 1745. Eight short months of campaigning north and south of the Border were to follow, only to end in disaster at Culloden.

(Location: On A830, 18 m W of Fort William, Lochaber, Highland Region.)

Crunchy Prawns

*Prawns are among the numerous shellfish available in the waters around the
west coast of Scotland, and although now very popular, they were not
eaten in any quantity by Scots people in earlier times. This is a good
supper dish.*

Serves 2

1 small piece each of onion,
  carrot, celery
1 bay leaf
2 peppercorns
300 ml (½ pint) milk, warmed
25 g (1 oz) margarine
25 g (1 oz) plain flour
½ 5 ml spoon (½ teaspoon) dry
  mustard

225 g (8 oz) prawns (thawed, if
  using frozen ones)
salt and pepper
50 g (2 oz) pinhead or rough
  oatmeal
75 g (3 oz) mild Cheddar cheese,
  grated

INFUSE the onion, carrot, celery, bay leaf and peppercorns in the warm milk
for 10 minutes. Strain and reserve the liquor. Melt the margarine in a pan, add
the flour and mustard and cook for a minute, then gradually stir in the
flavoured milk. Bring to the boil and cook until thick. Add the prawns, taste
for seasoning and place in a greased ovenproof dish. Mix the oatmeal and
cheese together and sprinkle on top. Bake at 200°C, 400°F, Gas Mark 6 for 20
minutes or until golden brown.

Fishwife's Haddie

*Finnan haddock, named after the port of Findon, are whole fish, with the
head removed but the bones left in. They are split, brined and smoked
to a pale colour. No dye is used. 'Pales' are made from smaller fish
and have a shorter curing time than finnans. They are delicious cut in
pieces and fried with smoked bacon.*

Serves 2

2 large smoked haddock
50 g (2 oz) butter
salt and pepper

2 5 ml spoons (2 teaspoons)
  cornflour
500 ml (18 fl oz) milk

SKIN the fish and cut in neat pieces. Melt the butter in a pan and add the fish.
Sprinkle with salt and pepper and cover with a tight-fitting lid. Cook gently
for 5 minutes. Blend the cornflour with the milk and pour over the fish. Cook
gently for a further 5 minutes, shaking the pan from time to time. Arrange
the fish on a serving dish and pour over the sauce. A poached egg or 'daub' of
cream may be served with each portion.

The House of Dun

THE HOUSE OF DUN is an elegant Palladian house, overlooking Montrose Basin. It was built by William Adam in 1730 for David Erskine, Lord Dun, who was an ardent Jacobite, a Member of Parliament, and, later, a judge of the Court of Session. His kinsman, and gentleman architect, 'Bobbing John' Erskine (called that because he was apt to change sides rather frequently), advised Lord Dun that the newly commissioned house 'ought to have one or two handsome and tolerable large rooms for the master to entertain his friends upon occasion and where couples of young folk may dance when they have the mind to divert themselves at Peace, Yull and High Times'.

Many years later, in 1827, another Erskine, John Erskine Kennedy-Erskine, married Augusta, child of the Duke of Clarence (later William IV) and the actress Mrs Jordan. The House of Dun seems then to have come into its own with the Lady Augusta. She must have been an enchanting character, impulsively throwing open her bedroom windows to breathe in the scents of her beloved fields and woods; throwing her tapestries to her long-suffering cook, Pierre Bordeaux, for him to get on with the boring background bits, and searching the countryside for interesting wild flowers. The kitchen, with its rows of copper pans, is one of the features of the house.

One of the most charming rooms is the bedroom of the girl–the last of the Erskines of Dun–who, as Mrs Lovett, left the House of Dun to the National Trust for Scotland after her death in 1980. In her bedroom are the watercolours and poems of Violet Jacob, one of Lady Augusta's grand-daughters, and surely a kindred spirit.

In the courtyard at House of Dun are reconstructions of gardeners' and gamekeepers' bothies, a game larder, a hen-house and a room where one may watch a weaver still producing fine linen. There is also an attractive tea-room with good home baking.

(Location: On A935, 4 m W of Montrose, Angus, Tayside Region.)

Hurl Pot Salmon

Near the House of Dun in Angus flows the river South Esk, a well-known salmon river. Like all salmon rivers, the pools and beats have interesting and attractive names; one such on the South Esk is the Hurl Pot. This recipe is similar to an old recipe for salmon hash. The storytellers would have us believe that it was a popular dinner dish with the poorly paid booksellers' clerks in the various hostelries in the Old Town in Edinburgh.

Serves 6–8

1½ kg (3 lb) tail-end piece of
   salmon
salt and pepper
a pinch of ground mace or grate
   of nutmeg
2 15 ml (2 tablespoons) fresh
   chives, chopped

300 ml (½ pint) fish stock
300 ml (½ pint) dry white wine
2 15 ml spoons (2 tablespoons)
   parsley, chopped

PUT the fish in a pan and just cover with water. Bring to the boil. Reduce the heat and simmer for 5 minutes. Remove the fish but retain the liquor. Carefully skin and bone the fish and cut the flesh into chunks. Return it to the pan with salt, pepper, mace and chives. Pour over the fish stock and wine and simmer gently for 25 minutes. Scatter parsley over and serve either hot or cold. Variations include the addition of prawns, small mushrooms and a dash of anchovy essence.

The Georgian House

IT IS NOT the elegance of design alone, nor the seemliness of arch and astragal, pediment and stone that make a visit to Charlotte Square such a satisfying experience. Each visit excites this satisfaction. To the Scot particularly, appreciation and enjoyment mingle happily with pride in its wholeness.

The architect of Charlotte Square—Robert Adam—was born in Kirkcaldy in 1728. He studied at Edinburgh University before travelling in Italy and Dalmatia. Back home, he was appointed architect to the King. Register House, at the eastern end of Princes Street, the Old Quadrangle of Edinburgh University and Glasgow Royal Infirmary were built to his designs.

The Georgian House at No 7 Charlotte Square came into the care of the National Trust for Scotland in 1966, but it was John, Chief of Clan Lamont who bought the feu in 1796 and paid £1800 for it. The Square is not a museum; people earn their varied livings behind the doors of the Square and there is a constant coming and going of ordinary people. Before the Trust opened the Georgian House to the public it was the premises of the well-known Edinburgh firm of Whytock and Reid, makers of fine furniture and plenishings.

The National Trust for Scotland is fortunate in having men of deep and extensive knowledge and scholarship to advise and care for this heritage. The castles and little houses, the gardens and countryside reflect important aspects of the life of Scotland past and present but the Georgian House *is* Edinburgh, the capital city.

(Location: In Edinburgh's city centre, two minutes from West End.)

Newhaven Creams

This is a very old recipe and doubtless got its name from the fishing village, Newhaven, near Edinburgh. The fishwives, in their traditional colourful costumes came daily to the city to sell their fish.

Serves 2 (or 4 as a starter)

450 g (1 lb) smoked haddock, cooked and boned
125 g (4 oz) breadcrumbs
salt and pepper

125 g (4 oz) butter
450 ml (¾ pint) milk or a mixture of milk and cream
3 eggs, size 3

FLAKE the fish and mash lightly, add the breadcrumbs and season to taste. Melt the butter in the milk and pour over the fish and breadcrumbs mixture. Beat the eggs well and mix in thoroughly. Pour into 1 large or 4 small greased ramekin dishes and cover securely with foil. Steam for 30 minutes. Unmould carefully on to a hot plate and serve with parsley sauce or white sauce with some finely chopped sorrel. To make these little moulds even lighter, beat in the egg yolks and fold in the stiffly beaten whites.

Oyster Loaves

This is one of those delightful recipes with no specific quantities. As is said in Scotland 'just a tickie of this and a tickie of that'. A tickie is an old word for a little. But as a guideline reckon on 2 oysters per roll, and 2 rolls per person for a light lunch. This recipe works equally well with the less expensive prawns.

TAKE some French rolls and brown carefully in the oven to crisp them up. Remove the soft crumb from the inside. Stew some oysters in their own juice. Drain and reserve the liquor. Make a sauce with this liquid, a glass of dry white wine, some mace and ground nutmeg and some butter rolled in flour. Whisk this all well together and heat the oysters in it. Fill into the crisp rolls.

Plaice with Bananas

Bananas are rich in nutrients and vitamins and complement the plaice perfectly in this unusual combination of flavours.

Serves 4

4 small plaice
seasoned flour
125 g (4 oz) butter
4 small bananas, peeled

juice of 1 lemon
4 5ml spoons (4 teaspoons) honey
fresh dill, chopped, and grated
   lemon rind, to garnish

Toss each plaice in flour which has been seasoned with salt, pepper and a little dill. Melt the butter in a shallow ovenproof dish and place the fish in the hot butter. Spoon over a little of the butter, cover the dish and bake at 190°C, 375°F, Gas Mark 5 for 20 minutes. Cut the bananas in half lengthwise, sprinkle with the lemon juice and honey and place in the dish with the fish. Bake for a further 5 minutes. Garnish with the rest of the dill and the finely grated lemon rind.

Scallops with Mushrooms

There are two main sizes and kinds of scallops: the King and the Queenie. Recently a new name has been found for the smaller 'Queenies': the Princess scallop. Scallops are normally harvested by dredging muddy and sandy seabeds but great progress has been made on the west coast of Scotland in farming these delicious shellfish. Because they are difficult to transport, some are cooked and prepared at the point of landing and the others rushed by express transport to the major markets in Britain and Europe.

Serves 6

6 large scallops
some milk
salt and pepper
2 15 ml spoons (2 tablespoons)
   white sauce

6 large mushrooms
25 g (1 oz) butter

REMOVE the scallops from their shells and wash well in cold water. Put in a pan with enough milk to cover. Add salt and pepper and simmer for 50 minutes. Do not allow to boil. Drain well. Chop the red and white parts of the scallops separately. Moisten each with white sauce and keep warm. Wipe the mushrooms and remove the stalks. Fry quickly in hot butter and place on serving plates. Put equal amounts of white scallop on each mushroom and top with the red part. Serve at once.

Smokie Mousse

Smokies are a speciality of the east coast town of Arbroath. The whole haddock has head and gut removed but it is not split. They are tied in pairs, hung on rods and hot smoked over hardwood chips till cooked. They can be grilled or eaten cold.

Serves 8

1 pair large smokies
2 5 ml spoons (2 teaspoons)
   gelatine

2 large packets cream cheese
a dash of dry sherry
3 egg whites, stiffly beaten

Mayonnaise
1 egg plus 3 yolks
2 5ml spoons (2 teaspoons) dry
   mustard
1 15 ml spoon (1 tablespoon)
   white wine vinegar

rind and juice of 1 lemon
a pinch of sugar
300 ml (½ pint) olive oil or corn
   oil (approx)
salt and pepper

FLAKE the flesh from the smokies and mash with a fork. To make the mayonnaise put the whole egg, 3 yolks, mustard, vinegar, rind and juice of the lemon and sugar into a blender. Blend, slowly adding enough oil until thick and creamy. Taste for seasoning. Dissolve the gelatine according to the instructions on the packet. Blend the cream cheese until smooth. Mix the cheese into the smokies with mayonnaise. Add sherry and gelatine, then fold in the stiffly beaten egg whites. Place in 8 small dishes or a fish mould and leave to set. Serve with small oatcakes.

Soused Herring

Herring, salted and cured, were for centuries the staple diet of many Scots people. The herring were soaked overnight in fresh water to remove some of the salt and boiled next day in a pan with potatoes to make the dish known as 'Tatties an' Herrin''.

Serves 3

6 herring
salt and pepper
approx 300 ml (½ pint) mixture
    water and white wine vinegar
    (roughly ⅔ water and ⅓
    vinegar)

4 bay leaves
1 15 ml spoon (1 tablespoon)
    pickling spices
2 small onions, thinly sliced

IF necessary, scale, clean and bone the herring. Season well with salt and pepper and roll up the fillets, skin side out, from the tail end. Place neatly and close together in an ovenproof dish. Pour over the water and vinegar mixture, add the bay leaves and pickling spices. Top with the onion slices. Cover closely and bake slowly at 150°C, 300°F, Gas Mark 2 for approximately 1 hour. Leave to cool in the liquid. Serve cold with salad.

Brodick Castle

THE ISLE OF ARRAN's shores, opposite the Ayrshire coast, provided good shelter for Viking galleys and even acted as a stepping stone for their invasion of Scotland. Much later, in 1306, Robert the Bruce watched from the island for the beacon fires on the mainland signalling that the time was ripe for him to begin his task of winning back Scotland. Still later, through the marriage of James, Lord Hamilton, and the daughter of James II of Scotland, much of Arran, including Brodick, passed to the Hamilton family. The castle was to remain a seat of the Hamiltons until the death of the twelfth Duke in 1895.

After the Civil War in the seventeenth century, peace reigned and people could get on with their lives without fear of losing their heads. In 1810 Brodick Castle was home to the tenth Duke of Hamilton who married Susan Beckford, heiress to great wealth. Their son married Princess Marie of Baden, cousin to Napoleon III. In 1906 Lady Mary Louise Hamilton, only child of the twelfth Duke, married the Duke of Montrose and, until the castle passed to the National Trust for Scotland in 1958, Brodick was a family seat of the Montrose family.

Although the castle is a treasure-house of rare and beautiful objects, the atmosphere is not that of a museum; rather one feels one is visiting friends. There is a warmth and domesticity in the midst of grandeur. In the Drawing Room, the chandelier hanging there came from Buchanan Castle, formerly a Montrose seat near Drymen, but now a ruin.

The world-famous gardens at Brodick reflect the care and skill of a family's devotion, and give pleasure to countless visitors. The Country Park in the castle grounds, Scotland's only island Country Park, and the mountain of Goatfell, provide recreation all the year round through the Ranger Service and help to protect the abundant wildlife.

(Location: Isle of Arran, 55-minute ferry from Ardrossan, connecting
bus to castle, 2 m.)

Viking Cod with Skirlie

Mrs Elizabeth Clelland, who wrote the New and Easy Method of Cookery *in 1759, recommended that 'the cod be served with a jug of melted butter with mustard in it and another jug with melted butter and anchovies'. Skirlie was often called 'Skirl-n-the-Pan' and is mentioned in Scott's* Old Mortality. *The name came from the 'skirl' or noise made by the hot fat when the onions were added. It can be served with any meat, game or fish dish.*

Serves 4

4 cod steaks
4–6 sprigs parsley, stalks left on
300 ml (½ pint) milk
300 ml (½ pint) water
salt and pepper

2 15 ml (2 tablespoons) butter
1½ 15 ml spoons (1½ tablespoons) flour
2 15 ml spoons (2 teaspoons) rough grain Arran mustard

Skirlie

125 g (4 oz) grated suet or 4 15 ml spoons (4 tablespoons) dripping
2 medium onions, finely chopped

225 g (8 oz) medium oatmeal or a mixture of medium and pinhead
salt and pepper

PUT the fish in a pan on top of the parsley to prevent it from sticking. Add the milk and water and a little salt. Cover and simmer gently for about 10 minutes, depending on the thickness of the fish, turning once to ensure even cooking. Remove to a warm serving dish and keep warm. Reserve the stock. To make the skirlie, put the suet or dripping into a hot pan and, when melted, add the onions and lighly brown them. Add the oatmeal and stir over a gentle heat for 5–10 minutes until cooked. Add salt and pepper to taste. Melt the butter, stir in the flour and mustard and gradually add the hot fish stock. Stir until it becomes creamy. Add pepper to taste and serve to accompany the cod, together with the skirlie.

MEAT
and
POULTRY
LARDER

Some hae meat and canna eat,
And some wad eat that want it:
But we hae meat and we can eat
Sae let the Lord be thankit.

THE SELKIRK GRACE   Robert Burns

S COTLAND is famous for its quality beef and lamb reared on the hills and
pastures, but Scots were not great meat eaters. They limited their
consumption to an ox or cattle beast killed at Martinmas (11 November) or to
the older sheep no longer of use for breeding. Today it is difficult to obtain
mutton – it has all become lamb!

Domestic poultry was an important part of the economy as, apart from
being a source of food, it was also used as payment for rent or services. Many
a Scots doctor has lived on chickens and eggs in payment for his services!

Many of the traditional meat and poultry dishes are of the casserole type,
showing the use of cheaper cuts of meat and older, less tender birds, cooked
for a long time over a slow heat. Full use was made of all the animal and many
tasty dishes were concocted from the offal – perhaps the best known being the
haggis: 'Great Chieftain o' the Puddin' Race', as Robert Burns described it.

At the Bachelors' Club at Tarbolton, Ayrshire, where Burns learned to dance, the annual Burns Supper with haggis is one of the highlights of the village calendar. And at Gladstone's Land, in the Royal Mile of Edinburgh, there is a model pig in its sty on the pavement to remind visitors that in the seventeenth century animals were kept for food in the city. Today the Trust maintains a 2685-acre farm on the Isle of Canna, with Highland cattle and sheep.

Boiled Gigot of Mutton and Caper Sauce

Although mutton, mature sheep, is not readily available in butchers' shops, year-old lambs can be used for this recipe. It is important not to use the young spring lamb as it is too tender and would be spoiled in the long cooking. The term 'gigot', the French word for a leg of meat, is an indication of the French influence on Scottish cooking.

Serves 6–8

1 leg of mutton about 2 kg (4½ lb)	*Caper Sauce*
milk	2 15 ml spoons (2 tablespoons) butter
2 large carrots, sliced	2 15 ml spoons (2 tablespoons) flour
2 large onions, sliced	900 ml (1½ pints) lamb stock
1 sprig each rosemary, thyme and parsley	3 15 ml spoons (3 tablespoons) capers and a little of their juice
salt and pepper	salt and pepper

REMOVE excess fat from the mutton and place the joint in a large pan. Pour in enough milk, or water and milk mixed, to come about three-quarters of the way up the joint. Add the carrots, onions and herbs and season well. Bring gently to the boil and skim well. Simmer gently for 2–3 hours until the meat is tender. To make the sauce, in another pan melt the butter and add the flour, cook for a minute and carefully add the lamb stock from the cooking pan. Add the capers and juice and cook until creamy. Season. Carve the mutton on a hot dish and pour over the sauce. Serve it with small boiled potatoes and small rounds of carrots which have been cooked in water and honey with mint. Sprinkle fresh chopped parsley over the meat.

Drum Castle

THE REMARKABLE THING about Drum Castle, near Aberdeen, is that for over 600 years, both in good times and bad, it was the home of one family–the Irvines. Throughout the world, wherever members of the family have gone, they have made a significant contribution to society. Just one example–in the nineteenth century, in Granada, Andalucia, lived and wrote Washington Irvine, creator of Rip van Winkle. In 1987 an exhibition about the Irvine family, partially financed by Clan Irvine of America, was created at Drum.

The original square keep was built about 1286 and used as a hunting tower by William the Lion and Alexander III. The de Irwins and the Bruce family came originally from Dumfriesshire and when Robert the Bruce began his campaign to win Scotland, the de Irwins were early followers. William de Irwin was later rewarded with the estate of Drum, including the power of 'pit and gallows'.

Wealth and possessions accrued and in the seventeenth century it was reported that 'they could ride all the way to Dundee on their own land'. During the Civil War, Drum's prosperity was destroyed. The Duke of Argyll turned the tenth Laird's wife and daughter out 'with nothing but two grey plaids and a couple of work nags'.

In the nineteenth century, the nineteenth Laird inherited his mother's estate of Schivas and he changed his name to Alexander Forbes Irvine, to include her maiden name. Thereafter the family were peace-loving worthy law-givers, soldiers and civil servants.

The property was given to the Trust in 1975. The old walled garden is now being redeveloped to create a special garden of historic roses, which grow so well in the neighbourhood, and there is a Trust tea-room in the castle.

(Location: Off A93, 10 m W of Aberdeen, Kincardine and Deeside, Grampian.)

Braised Shoulder of Lamb

*Braising is a popular French method of cooking the less tender cuts of meat;
it is a cross between roasting and stewing. Any selection of vegetables may be
used and the gravy thickened slightly with some cornflour, if liked.*

Serves 6–8

3–4 15 ml spoons
  (3–4 tablespoons) oil
2–2.5 kg (4½–5½ lb) shoulder of
  lamb
2 large carrots

2 onions
2 sticks celery
salt and pepper
450 ml (¾ pint) water or stock

HEAT the oil in a large pan and brown the lamb well on all sides. Remove and
lay aside. Add the carrots, onions and celery, cut into large chunks, and allow
them to brown for 5–10 minutes. Place them in an ovenproof casserole, just
large enough to hold the lamb, and put the lamb on top. Season well. Add the
stock to the pan and boil up with the rich pan juices, pour over the meat and
add enough extra liquid to come halfway up the lamb. Cover tightly and
cook at 170°C, 325°F, Gas Mark 3 for about 1½ hours until the meat is nearly
tender. Remove the lid and increase the heat to 230°C, 450°F, Gas Mark 8 for
about 15–20 minutes to crisp the top. Remove the meat and serve with some
of the vegetables and the gravy.

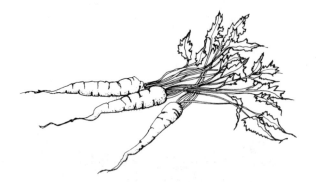

Chicken with Gooseberries

*Honey was important as a sweetener before sugar became easily available.
The Scots were keen beekeepers and the honey from the bees which had
spent the summer among the heather on the hills had a special flavour.
Gooseberries for cooking should be green and small and are generally much
sourer than the yellow and red dessert berries. The tang of the berries and the
sweetness of the honey give the chicken a delicious taste.*

Serves 4–6

600 ml (1 pint) chicken stock
300 ml (½ pint) dry white wine
1 blade mace
salt and pepper
1 chicken about 1.5–2 kg (3–4 lb)

Sauce
2 large egg yolks
1–2 slices bread
3 15 ml spoons (3 tablespoons)
   cider vinegar
1 5 ml spoon (1 teaspoon) honey
25 g (1 oz) butter
175 g (6 oz) stewed gooseberries

PUT the stock, wine and mace in a pan large enough to hold the chicken.
Season the inside of the chicken with salt and pepper and place in the pan.
Bring to the boil and simmer over a low heat till tender–about 45 minutes.
Remove the chicken from the pan, reserving the stock, and carve into
portions. Put these on a serving dish and keep warm. To make the sauce, beat
the egg yolks in a bowl and carefully beat in approximately 300 ml (½ pint) of
the hot chicken stock and return it to the pan. Crumble in the bread and stir
over a low heat until the sauce thickens but do not let it boil or it will curdle.
Add the cider vinegar, honey, butter and gooseberries. Heat gently and pour
over the chicken.

Collops in the Pan

This recipe is a perfect example of the simplicity of Scottish cooking. It is thought that 'collop' may be from the French escalope, *meaning a thin steak and shows yet again the association between France and Scotland.*

Serves 8

2 15 ml spoons (2 tablespoons)
   butter
8 thin slices rump steak, about
   5 mm (¼ in) thick
4 medium onions, sliced

salt and black pepper
1 15 ml spoon (1 tablespoon)
   walnut, mushroom or oyster
   ketchup

MELT the butter in a heavy pan and when hot add the meat. Sear it well on both sides and add the onions. Season well. Cover and cook gently for 10 minutes. Remove and place on a hot serving dish. Add the chosen ketchup to the pan juices and bring to the boil. Pour over the steaks and serve at once.

Dubton Pie

This is a good example of how the thrifty Scots housewife would 'stretch' or extend a recipe to feed any extra mouths. Sometimes diced carrots and turnips would be added to the mince mixture, making it go even further and also saving on fuel.

Serves 4

450 g (1 lb) steak, minced
1 small onion
2 5 ml spoons (2 teaspoons)
   oatmeal
salt and pepper
150 ml (¼ pint) beef stock
dash of mushroom ketchup

Topping
50 g (2 oz) margarine
150 g (5 oz) self-raising flour
salt and pepper
a pinch of mixed herbs
2 eggs, well beaten
1 15 ml spoon (1 tablespoon)
   medium oatmeal

PUT an empty pan on to heat and when hot add the minced steak. Break it down with a wooden spoon and let it brown well in its own fat. Add the onion and brown it. Stir in the oatmeal and seasoning. Mix well and add the stock and ketchup. Cover and cook gently for about 30 minutes, checking if more stock is required as the finished mince must not be too thick. To make the topping, rub the margarine into the flour, season and add the herbs, then mix in the eggs to give a soft batter-like dough. Put the mince in an ovenproof dish, spread the topping over, sprinkle with medium oatmeal and bake at 190°C, 375°F, Gas Mark 5 for 45 minutes. Serve with mashed turnips.

Culloden Battlefield

THE SAD, ROMANTIC figure of Prince Charles Edward Stuart is still a controversial one. On one side is his legendary courage and charm; on the other his inexperience of politics and the bad counsel he listened to which helped to bring about the disaster of Culloden. Had the Prince continued his march to London from Derby or managed to attack Cumberland as he lay at Nairn, things might have been different.

But on 16 April 1746 at Culloden, on bleak Drumossie Moor, the Prince's army of less than 5000 men fought the government force of 9000 troops led by the Duke of Cumberland. In a fierce battle lasting less than an hour the Jacobite cause was lost for ever.

Retribution was savagely meted out by the government troops who hunted down anyone who had had a part in the '45, and hundreds who had had no real part at all. The old order of life in the Highlands was never the same again.

For the following five months when the Prince sought refuge in remote corners of the Highlands and islands, £30,000, a huge sum in those days, was offered for his capture. But not one whisper of betrayal sullied the total loyalty of his supporters. At last, on 19 September 1746, the frigate *L'Heureux* sailed from Loch nan Uamh, near Glenfinnan, and bore the Prince away from Scotland.

> Bonnie Charlie's noo awa'
> Safely ower the friendly main.
> Mony a heart will break in twa
> Should he ne'er come back again.

The battlefield of Culloden has been restored to its original moorland by the Trust and there is an interpretive centre with an exhibition about the battle, an audio-visual presentation in various languages and a fine restaurant with home baking.

(Location: On B9006, 5 m E of Inverness, Highland Region.)

Fitless Cock

Religion played an important part in the life of the Scots people and the Fitless, or Fastyn, Cock was eaten on the evening of the day before the start of Lent. In the south of Scotland a similar dish was called Dry Goose. In the years of the Second World War (1939–45), when meat was rationed, many a Scots housewife would serve Fitless Cock on one of the meatless days each week.

Serves 4

225 g (8 oz) oatmeal, toasted in
  the oven until nutty
125 g (4 oz) beef suet (use the
  commercial shredded kind)

1 onion, finely chopped
salt and black pepper
beaten egg to bind

MIX all the ingredients together and mould into the shape of a fowl or into an oval. Scald a clean pudding cloth, flour it well and place the oatmeal mixture in the centre. Tie securely, leaving room for expansion, and cook in a pan of boiling water for 2 hours. (It can also be steamed in a bowl over hot water.)

Friar's Chicken

Mrs Hanna Glasse, who lived in London and who wrote The Art of Cookery Made Plain and Easy *in 1747, called this dish 'Scots Chicken' and commented that 'it was a pretty dish for sick people'. The origin of the dish is veiled in mystery but perhaps it was one of the recipes brought back to Scotland by the intrepid travellers of the eighteenth century. It should be served in the old-fashioned deep soup plates found in most Scots kitchens.*

Serves 6

1 chicken about 1.5–2 kg (3–4 lb)
chicken stock
1 small onion, finely chopped
salt and pepper

1 15 ml spoon (1 tablespoon)
  parsley, chopped
3 eggs, well beaten

JOINT the chicken and place in a pan with enough hot stock to cover, and add the onion and seasoning. Simmer gently until tender – about 45–60 minutes. Add the parsley. Carefully stir 2–3 15 ml spoons (2–3 tablespoons) of the hot stock into the eggs, mix well and return to the pan. Stir well, and heat through but do not allow to boil or the eggs will curdle. Serve the pieces of chicken in a deep plate with the broth poured over.

Glencoe

SUCH A WILD DRAMATIC place as Glencoe has inevitably hosted wild dramatic events. And yet, throughout its turbulent history when family feuds often led to bitter skirmishes, the common folk got on with their agriculture peacefully enough. They had reasonably fertile land, there were fish in the burns and lochs and their sheep, though small, provided wool and meat. However, cattle rustling was a favourite occupation for generations, and raid after raid ended in blood and recrimination.

The infamous massacre of Glencoe took place in February 1692 and was the culmination not only of clan bitterness, but also of the base machinations of government men. Some Highland clans were reluctant to acknowledge William III as their King. Among them was Alastair, the twelfth chief of the Macdonalds of Glencoe. He tried to fulfil the order to swear allegiance by a certain date, but because of various treacherous delays failed to do so. Instructions were given for the indiscriminate butchery of the whole 'damnable tribe'. All passes were to be guarded so that none should escape: 'This is the proper season to maul them in the long dark nights.' And on 13 February 1692 a force of 130, led by Robert Campbell of Glen Lyon, slew 38 Macdonalds – men, women and children.

Glencoe now has a fine road running between the Aonach Eagach ridge and the sentinel mountains from Buachaille Etive Mor to Meall Mor. Drama lies nowadays in mountain climbing and ski-racing, but to the perceptive visitors, echoes of a painful past still linger in the sombre glen.

The Trust's visitor centre at the foot of the glen provides an excellent stopping-off point to see the view and to have a cup of tea in the snack bar.

(Location: On A82, 18 m S of Fort William, Lochaber.)

Pan Haggis

This is a less rich version of the traditional haggis and is both economical and nourishing. It is served with clapshot which is a native Orcadian dish: boiled potatoes and boiled turnip are mashed together with plenty of black pepper, a large knob of butter and with chopped chives added just before serving.

Serves 4

350 g (12 oz) ox liver, in one piece	1–2 onions
250 ml (9 fl oz) water	150 g (5 oz) oatmeal
salt and pepper	125 g (4 oz) beef suet

BOIL the liver in the water with some salt for 40 minutes. Reserve the liquor, or 'bree', and grate the liver on a coarse grater. Parboil the onions for 5 minutes and chop finely. Brown the oatmeal in a pan over a gentle heat to give it a rich nutty flavour. Mix the liver, onion, suet and oatmeal with enough liver bree to give a softish mixture. Season well and place in a greased pudding basin. Cover securely with greased paper or foil and steam for 2 hours. Serve hot with clapshot.

Potted Hough

Potting was a favourite way of preserving food in the short term in the eighteenth and nineteenth centuries. Gifts of potted meats and game were often sent to friends and were always eaten at New Year and on shooting-party lunches.

Serves 10–12

1½ kg (3 lb) hough or shin of beef	1 medium oxtail may be added to
1 nap or shin bone	make it richer
salt and pepper	water

PUT the hough, nap bone and some salt in a pan. If using oxtail, have the butcher joint it, and add to the pan. Just cover with cold water and bring slowly to the boil. Simmer gently for at least 4 hours (ideally put it in a slow oven overnight). Take all the meat off the bones, and chop or mince or shred it according to your own liking. Return the meat to the liquid in the pan and season well with salt and black pepper. Boil rapidly for 10 minutes only. Cool, remove any fat and pour into wetted moulds. Chill well before serving with boiled potatoes, pickled beetroot and redcurrant jelly. Care must be taken to keep it cool or the jelly will melt.

Salmagundi

According, once again, to Mrs Glasse in her famous book, this is 'a hotch potch of minced meats, game, eggs, herbs, vegetables and anchovies'. In other words it is a typical tasty Scots way of using up leftovers from an earlier meal. Any combination of meat, fish or vegetables can be used according to taste but it is important to garnish it well with the anchovies and egg.

Serves 6

6 15 ml spoons (6 tablespoons) mayonnaise
juice of ½ lemon
2 15 ml spoons (2 tablespoons) single cream
salt and pepper
125 g (4 oz) cooked ham, chopped
2 cooked chicken breasts, chopped

4 hard-boiled eggs, the whites chopped, the yolks sieved
2 small red apples, sliced with skin left on
3 sticks celery, chopped
4 syboes or spring onions, sliced
6 anchovy fillets

Mix together the mayonnaise, lemon juice and cream and season well. Mix the ham, chicken, egg whites, apples, celery and syboes together, then stir in the mayonnaise. Pile into a serving dish. Decorate with the anchovy fillets and egg yolks.

Small Mutton Pies

These are usually bakers' or butchers' pies but are easy to make and any filling can be used, such as lean steak, venison, chicken or a vegetarian mixture.

Serves 6

Filling
350 g (12 oz) lean lamb or mutton
1 small onion, finely chopped
salt and pepper
1–2 5 ml spoons (1–2 teaspoons)
   Worcester sauce
a little stock

Pastry
450 g (1 lb) plain flour
1 5 ml spoon (1 teaspoon) salt
150 g (5 oz) lard or dripping
300 ml (½ pint) water and milk
   mixed (half and half)

CHOP the meat and mix with the onion, salt and pepper and Worcester sauce in a pan over a low heat to draw the juices from the meat. Moisten with a little stock but do not make too wet. To make the pastry, mix the flour and salt in a bowl. Melt the fat in the water and milk to boiling point. Pour over the flour. Knead to a smooth dough and divide into one-third and two-thirds. Cut the larger piece into 6 and mould each round a straight-sided mould or tin. The cases should be about 4 cm (1½ in) deep and 7.5 cm (3 in) wide. Place on a baking sheet and fill with the meat mixture until about three-quarters full. Roll out the rest of the dough and cut 6 circles to fit the cases. Dampen the edges and cover the pies. Crimp the edges firmly and make 2 holes in the top to allow the steam to escape. Brush with a little milk and bake at 200°C, 400°F, Gas Mark 6 for 45 minutes. Serve hot with extra gravy, mashed potatoes and peas or beans.

Craigievar Castle

IT IS A CONTINUAL source of astonishment to realise just how much trade and cultural activity there was in times past between Scotland and the Continent, especially France, the Low Countries and Scandinavia. In the early days of the seventeenth century, William Forbes of Aberdeen had travelled a good deal. He had obtained his Master of Arts degree from Edinburgh University, married the Provost's daughter and gone on to establish lucrative trading with the Baltic countries–thence his nickname 'Danzig Willie'.

In 1610 he bought the unfinished Craigievar Castle, near Alford, from the Mortimer family and commissioned the best local workmen to complete the building. If Scotland was not rich in timber it was certainly rich in stone, and somehow the solidity of the stone building rising tall and narrow only to blossom out in happy curves, corbels and turrets, seems to emphasize the notion that perhaps there was not then so much need to build for defence. Timber was used economically inside the castle and the panelling is thought to have been done by local craftsmen. Later, skilled journeymen plasterers completed the internal decoration.

The family who owned the 'fairy-tale castle' of Craigievar throughout the years since 1610, the Forbes-Sempills, cared for it diligently and were happy there. Everywhere was the emblem of Craigievar–the 'cock proper'–seeming to shout from its pinnacle on the weathervane to all and sundry, 'Wha daur meddle wi' me?'

In 1963, the castle was presented to the Trust by a consortium of benefactors.

(Location: On A980, 26 m W of Aberdeen, Gordon, Grampian Region.)

Stoved Chicken

*This is a traditional method of cooking and is a variation of the famous
Stovies. There is some discussion as to its origin. Some say it is from the
French étuver—to sweat or cook in its own steam. Others say it is from the
old Scots and North of England word 'stove'—a closed box or vessel of
earthenwear, porcelain, or metal. Stovies, eaten at every Hogmanay party,
consist of sliced potatoes and sliced onions, browned in good beef dripping or
bacon fat and layered with plenty of seasoning and a little stock. Sometimes,
near the end of the cooking time, cooked chopped meat is added.*

Serves 8

1 chicken about 1½ kg (3 lb)
50 g (2 oz) butter or dripping
1 kg (2 lb) potatoes, peeled (old
   main crop, not small new ones)
2 large onions, sliced
salt and pepper

600 ml (1 pint) stock, made from
   the giblets of the chicken
3 15 ml spoons (3 tablespoons)
   parsley, chopped, or 2 of
   parsley and 1 of tarragon

JOINT the chicken and cut into large cubes. Melt half the butter or dripping in
a heavy pan or casserole. Add the chicken pieces and brown lightly. Remove
the pan from the heat and lift out the chicken. Cover the base of the casserole
with a layer of thickly sliced potatoes. Add a layer of onion and season well.
Add a layer of chicken, dotting each layer with butter or dripping. Continue
with layers, finishing with one of potatoes. Pour over the stock, cover tightly
and cook in a slow oven, 150°C, 300°F, Gas Mark 2 for about 2 hours or until
the chicken is tender. Add a little more stock after half the cooking time if
necessary. Sprinkle with the parsley just before serving.

GAME BAG

A man is in general better pleased when he has a good dinner on the table,
than when his wife talks Greek.

Samuel Johnson

SCOTLAND, a country of mountain, moor and forest, is a great natural
habitat for many species of game. Deer roam on the high hills, grouse
feed richly on heather-clad moors, while on the lower slopes the pheasant and
partridge have their nests. Rabbits and hares played an important part in the
diet of the Scots people. Many towns had special warrens for rabbits and a
Warrener appointed to look after them.

Pigeons were also a valuable source of food. They were reared and kept in
special houses known as dovecots or doocots. These were usually square or
oblong and had special landing ledges for the pigeons to sit on, protected
from the prevailing wind. Although many have fallen into ruin over the
centuries, the Trust has restored two, Phantassie Doocot at Preston Mill,
East Linton in East Lothian and Boath Doocot by Auldearn, Nairnshire.
Their main purpose was to provide a plentiful supply of fresh meat for the
people, but many farmers whose crops were eaten by these birds looked on
them with little favour. They were also a great nuisance as reported by the
church at Tyninghame in East Lothian, where the beadle was given an

allowance 'for pouther to shoot the doos for they file the seats i' the kirk'!
(Gunpowder to shoot the pigeons because they dirty the seats in the church.)

Game as we know it today was not shot for sport until the nineteenth
century when improved travel encouraged more people to come to Scotland
for the 'shooting' every autumn. The Gun Room, Fishing Room and Game
Larder at the House of Dun by Montrose in Angus have been faithfully
restored by the Trust and, with their old game books, provide an insight into
the sporting life of the district.

Casserole of Venison

*Venison is becoming increasingly popular and the advent of deer farming on
a large scale ensures a readily available supply of good quality meat.
Venison is the name given to the flesh of red deer, roe deer and fallow deer.
It is a relatively fat-free meat and is improved by marinading in oil and wine
before cooking.*

Serves 6–8

1.5 kg (3 lb) venison
2 large onions
2 large carrots
2 cloves garlic
60 ml (4 tablespoons) olive oil
½ bottle red wine

seasoned flour (salt, pepper and
  mixed herbs)
1 bay leaf
225 g (8 oz) mushrooms, chopped
150 ml (¼ pint) meat stock
salt and pepper

Cut the venison into cubes. Peel and chop 1 onion, 1 carrot and the garlic.
Place the meat and vegetables in a large bowl with the olive oil and stir well to
coat before adding the wine. Mix well, cover and allow to soak for 24 hours
in a cool place. Remove the venison from the marinade and toss it in seasoned
flour, reserving the marinade. Peel and chop the remaining onion and carrot
and fry in a little oil for 2–3 minutes. Transfer them to an ovenproof
casserole. Fry the venison cubes to a rich brown and add to the casserole. Add
the bay leaf and the mushrooms. Pour in the reserved marinade. Heat the
stock in the pan, scraping down any residue and add to the casserole. Season
well and simmer at 150°C, 300°F, Gas Mark 2 for 2–2½ hours. Serve with
baked or creamed potatoes and rowan jelly.

Crathes Castle

IN 1323, ALEXANDER BURNETT, or Burnard, received a gift of land at Banchory from Robert the Bruce in return for loyal service. With the land went the jewelled ivory horn, 'the Horn of Leys' as badge of his office, the Royal Forester of Drum.

For many years the Burnetts lived on an island, or crannog, in the middle of the Loch of Leys and it was not until the end of the sixteenth century, at a time when the defence of one's home was not such an important priority, that Alexander and his wife, Katherine Gordon, moved into their new castle at Crathes, with its marvellous painted ceilings depicting great heroes of the past. These figures come alive in their bright blues, reds and terracottas, with inscriptions such as 'Hop is a vertue of cingular grace'.

The next laird was Sir Thomas, who was at odds with the reforms being promulgated by the Catholic King, Charles I. So, too, initially was Montrose, but he subsequently became the King's lieutenant in Scotland. When Montrose's army camped outside Crathes and demanded peaceful surrender, Sir Thomas complied and that night the two friends dined together in the great hall of the castle.

The great gardens at Crathes are the inspired work of generations of committed gardeners, while beyond lies the parkland rich in wildlife and woodland paths.

(Location: On A93 15 m W of Aberdeen, Kincardine and Deeside, Grampian.)

Cranberried Pheasant Breasts

The Romans are said to have brought the pheasant to Britain from Greece where it was known as the Phasian bird. It has a less strong flavour than grouse.

Serves 4

25 g (1 oz) butter
4 breasts of pheasants (use the
   carcases and legs for stock)
½ onion or 1 shallot, finely
   chopped
25 g (1 oz) plain flour

300 ml (½ pint) jellied game stock
salt, pepper and mixed herbs
1 small can cranberry sauce (or
   fresh cranberries, if available)
4 15 ml spoons (4 tablespoons)
   double cream

MELT the butter in a flameproof casserole and brown the pheasant breasts. Remove from the pan and fry the onion or shallot. Add the flour and brown it. Pour in the stock, bring to the boil and season to taste with salt, pepper and herbs. Add the pheasant and cranberry sauce. Cover and cook at 180°C, 350°F, Gas Mark 4 for about 1½ hours or until tender. Remove the pheasant breasts to a warm serving dish and keep hot. Sieve or liquidize the sauce, add the cream and heat through without boiling. Pour over the pheasant and serve.

Gallowe's Knowe Game Pie

This pie takes its name from an area at House of Dun and is a delicious one which can be made with any variety of game. We will not dwell on the function of a site called Gallowe's Knowe but just enjoy the pie!

Serves 6–8

Filling
1 young pheasant or 4 pheasant
    legs
2 chicken breasts or legs
225 g (8 oz) smoked streaky bacon
1 small onion, chopped
salt and pepper
1 15 ml spoon (1 tablespoon)
    parsley, chopped
a pinch of dried thyme
2 5 ml spoons (2 teaspoons)
    gelatine

300 ml (½ pint) game stock

Pastry
450 g (1 lb) plain flour
1 5 ml spoon (1 teaspoon) salt
150 g (5 oz) lard
300 ml (½ pint) milk and water
    mixed (half and half)
beaten egg, to glaze

REMOVE all the meat from the game and chicken and chop fairly small. Chop the bacon and add to the meat with the chopped onion, seasoning and herbs. Mix well. Make the pastry by mixing the flour and salt in a bowl. Melt the lard in the milk and water mixture to boiling point and pour on to the flour. Mix quickly into a dough. Use three-quarters of it to line a 20 cm (8 in) round cake tin or a 1 kg (2 lb) loaf tin, preferably one with a loose base or lined with foil. Spoon the filling into the pastry case and cover with the rest of the pastry. Seal the edges well and decorate with any scraps of pastry. Crimp the edges firmly and make 2 holes on top to allow the steam to escape. Glaze with beaten egg and bake at 200°C, 400°F, Gas Mark 6 for 30 minutes. Reduce the heat to 180°C, 350°F, Gas Mark 4. Glaze the pie again and bake for a further 1¼–1½ hours. If the pie is browning too much, cover it with a piece of foil. Allow to cool. Dissolve the gelatine in the game stock, season and pour into the pie through a funnel inserted in the holes on top. Chill thoroughly and serve cold.

Poacher's Stewpot

Rabbit, once again available from most butchers, makes an excellent stew or casserole. The poachers of old times knew how to make the most of the food 'available' and any variety of game would probably go into the stewpot.

Serves 8

15 g (½ oz) lard or dripping
225 g (8 oz) streaky bacon, chopped
1 large onion, peeled and cut into chunks
2 sticks celery, cut into pieces

1 kg (2 lb) rabbit cut into pieces
25 g (1 oz) plain flour
300 ml (½ pint) brown ale
300 ml (½ pint) stock
salt and pepper

HEAT the lard in a large flameproof casserole and fry the bacon, onion and celery until brown. Coat the rabbit in flour, add to the casserole and brown well. Add the ale and stock, and season well. Cover and cook in the oven at 190°C, 375°F, Gas Mark 5 for about 1 hour or until tender. If liked, dumplings may be added for the last 25 minutes of cooking.

Dumplings

125 g (4 oz) self-raising flour
40 g (1½ oz) suet
1 15 ml spoon (1 tablespoon) parsley, chopped

½ 5 ml spoon (½ teaspoon) dried thyme
salt and pepper
40–60 ml (3–4 tablespoons) water

MIX all the ingredients together, then divide into 8. Shape into balls and add to the casserole. (If liked they may be tossed in pinhead oatmeal before adding to the stew.) A little more stock may be needed when dumplings are added.

Fyvie Castle

THE HISTORY OF FYVIE Castle, a few miles from Turriff, Grampian, goes back to the thirteenth century when it was a royal stronghold. Robert the Bruce, in his day, is said to have meted out justice under the trees there. There are five towers of Fyvie; one of them, the Seton tower at the centre of the south front, reminds us that Sir Alexander Seton was a godson of Mary Queen of Scots; his cousin Mary was one of the 'four Maries' of the sad and tender song.

Portraits by Raeburn are memorable features of Fyvie and a painting by Batoni of William Gordon is particularly outstanding. William Gordon was nephew to Lord Lewis Gordon, of Jacobite fame, who stayed at Fyvie before setting out on the march to join Prince Charles Edward at Perth. In 1746 William stood with his mother to watch 'Butcher' Cumberland pass on his way to Culloden. Cumberland gave the boy an orange, the symbol of the Whigs, hoping he 'would one day prove as loyal an adherent to the House of Hanover as your uncle has been to the House of Stuart'.

While the last of the Gordons was at Fyvie, there lived nearby Admiral John Leith who was married to Margaret Forbes, a descendant of Sir Henry Preston of Fyvie. Their son Alexander joined the navy and found himself in San Francisco where he met and married in 1871 Marie Louise January, an American heiress. Outside the walls of the Gallery at Fyvie are their initials and the words 'Gang East and West, But Hame's Best'.

There is a charming story of how Queen Victoria Eugenie of Spain, granddaughter of Queen Victoria, spent part of her honeymoon at Fyvie. It was not the custom in Spain for a Queen to be seen dancing in public and so her husband, the King, demurred. 'You can refuse me nothing on my honeymoon,' said the Queen and to the skirl of the pipes and the astonishment of the Spanish courtiers, she danced the night away.

Today, the old kitchen has been converted into a Trust tea-room where the quality of the home baking draws many visitors.

(Location: Off A947, 25 m NW of Aberdeen, Grampian.)

Pupton of Pigeons

This recipe is given as a piece of history. It is very rich and so perhaps not to be eaten too often in our cholestorol-conscious age. The same filling could be put into a pasty or pie made with a shortcrust pastry.

Serves 4–6

Forcemeat
175 g (6 oz) cooked lamb
125 g (4 oz) dripping
salt and pepper
½ 5 ml spoon (½ teaspoon) each
  nutmeg, ground mace and
  lemon peel
2 egg yolks
225 g (8 oz) soft white
  breadcrumbs
beaten egg to glaze

Filling
2 cooked pigeon breasts, sliced
  (use the rest for the stock pot)
175 g (6 oz) cooked lamb, sliced
4 slices streaky bacon, diced
75 g (3 oz) mushrooms
2 hard-boiled egg yolks

MAKE the forcemeat first. Mince the lamb with the dripping or use a processor to make a smooth paste. Add the seasoning, spices and lemon peel, egg yolks and enough breadcrumbs to give a firm dough. Roll out half to line a 20 cm (8 in) dish. (If it is too crumbly, press the mixture round the sides of the dish.) Sprinkle a little flour on the base and layer in the pigeon, lamb and bacon. Fill in the spaces with mushrooms. Top with the crumbled hard-boiled egg yolk and a little flour. Add seasoning and cover with the rest of the forcemeat. Glaze the top with beaten egg and bake at 180°C, 350°F, Gas Mark 4 for 30–35 minutes until the crust is crisp and brown. Serve with gravy and green cabbage.

Roast Grouse

A native of Scotland, this little bird does not survive well in other countries.
The red grouse is the most common and is considered a great delicacy. It
is in season from August to December. It needs only the simplest cooking
to bring out its full distinctive flavour. Older, tougher birds enhance a
game casserole or pie.

Serves 2

2 young grouse
50 g (2 oz) softened butter
salt and pepper

4 slices fat bacon
1 15 ml spoon (1 tablespoon) oil

THE legs are often removed from the grouse before roasting as they have a slightly bitter flavour. They can be used in the game stock pot for soup or gravy. Divide the butter in two pieces and insert a piece into each bird. Season lightly. Lay a piece of bacon over each bird. Heat the oil in a roasting tin and add the birds, coating them well in the hot oil. Roast at 230°C, 450°F, Gas Mark 8 for about 15 minutes. Remove the bacon and return to the oven for about 10 minutes to brown. Serve on a croûte of toast or fried bread with a garnish of watercress. Traditional accompaniments to roast grouse are rowan jelly and game chips.

Leith Hall

NOWADAYS THE SUCCESS of agriculture in Aberdeenshire is famous and taken for granted, but it was not always so. Dr Johnson pronounced the countryside around to be 'bleak and barren'. However, Scotland has long been fortunate in rearing men of vision and energy who helped to establish a more prosperous way of life, and the family connected with Leith Hall was of that number.

Apart from their agricultural activities, the Leiths, the Hays and their successors, the Leith-Hays, had strong military connections which are highlighted in the house in an exhibition, 'For Crown and Country: the Military Lairds of Leith Hall'. Andrew Hay marched to Derby and back with Bonnie Prince Charlie. Still to be seen in the house is the rare pardon written in 1780 by George III, allowing Andrew Hay to return from over forty years' exile. He was able to help the family out of financial difficulty and his name is important in the history of Leith Hall. With the estate more stable, the Leiths were able to turn their attentions ever more to the army, politics and empire.

General Sir James Leith, perhaps the family's most distinguished soldier, commanded the 5th Division under Wellington in Spain, and was involved in the siege of San Sebastian. He is buried in Westminster Abbey. His great-nephew Sebastian was in the Thin Red Line at Balaclava and led the 93rd Sutherland Highlanders to the relief of Lucknow. Of course, as always, there were valiant and competent women at home holding the fort and completing some beautiful needlework that hangs in the passages.

A feature of the estate is the unique eighteenth-century curved stable block. The grounds offer woodland walks, a bird observation hide, an ice house, unusual animals and a beautiful garden. There is an attractive Trust tea-room in the old kitchen.

(Location: On B9002, 34 m NW of Aberdeen, Grampian.)

Venison Picnic Parcels

*This uses the liver and less tender neck meat in a delicious savoury bundle
which is equally at home on a picnic or a buffet.*

Makes 20

450 g (1 lb) venison liver
450 g (1 lb) neck meat of venison
225 g (8 oz) onions, peeled
225 g (8 oz) breadcrumbs
2 5 ml spoons (2 teaspoons) salt
  and pepper mixed

½ 5 ml spoon (½ teaspoon) sage
3 good pinches thyme
1 egg, beaten
450 g (1 lb) smoked streaky bacon

MINCE the liver, neck meat and onions and place in a large bowl with the
breadcrumbs. Add the seasoning and herbs and mix well with egg to bind.
Form into 20 balls, wrap in bacon and secure with a wooden cocktail stick.
Place in a well-greased baking tin and bake at 200°C, 400°F, Gas Mark 6 for
40–45 minutes. Serve hot or cold with brown bread and butter.

KITCHEN GARDEN

Happy is the family which can eat onions together. They are, for the time being, separate from the world and have a harmony of aspiration.
MY SUMMER IN A GARDEN, Charles Warner, 1871

ALTHOUGH the Scots have always had the reputation of not eating many vegetables except as part of another dish, such as Scotch Broth, this is not wholly true. In certain areas where the soil was thin and not fertile, they would be limited to kail, turnips and possibly potatoes; but in the rich fertile lands around Glasgow, in Midlothian and in Morayshire, many of the vegetables which we eat today were grown and enjoyed. Monks were responsible for bringing new vegetables and fruits to Scotland from Europe and their skill as gardeners was passed down to the lay workers in the monasteries. They in turn trained others in the art of gardening.

In 1683 the first comprehensive book on gardening was published by John Reid. He not only gave instructions on how to grow vegetables, such as lettuce, broccoli, spinach, asparagus and numerous herbs, but also gave strict orders on how to prepare and cook them! As freshness is of paramount importance in cooking it is equally so in selecting vegetables. There is only one place for old, wilted vegetables—the dustbin or the compost heap. Today we can still, in some areas, buy direct from farm shops or market stalls.

The walled vegetable garden at Inverewe Garden in Wester Ross is an additional attraction for the many thousands of visitors who flock there to see the famous rhododendrons and azaleas. And at Culzean Country Park in Ayrshire the Trust has a fine exhibition telling the story of agrarian reform in Scotland at the end of the seventeenth century.

Asparagus and Cauliflower Salad

The famous gardener, John Reid, considered the kitchen garden 'to be the best of all gardens' and saw it as a sheltered walled place where it was possible to grow more unusual crops such as asparagus, artichokes and spinach.

30 asparagus tips, cooked
1 cauliflower, lightly cooked, but
  still firm

mayonnaise or other preferred
  dressing, such as remoulade

BREAK the cauliflower into small florets and mix with the asparagus. Pour over the dressing and serve at once.

Beetroot and Celery Salad

The various colours and textures in this salad make it attractive to look at and good to eat.

125 g (4 oz) cooked beetroot (do
  not use beetroot in vinegar)
1 large celery stick
1 orange
1 red-skinned dessert apple
1 small head chicory

Dressing
20 ml (4 teaspoons) lemon juice
10 ml (2 teaspoons) olive or
  sunflower oil
mustard
salt and pepper
1 15 ml spoon (1 tablespoon)
  chopped chives

CUT the beetroot into small cubes. Chop the celery finely. Peel and slice the orange and cut in quarters. Remove the core from the apple and cut into small cubes. Arrange the chicory head leaves round the dish, and pile the beetroot, celery, orange and apple into the centre. Mix all the dressing ingredients in a screw-top jar and shake well before pouring over the salad.

Chicory and Citrus Salad

The tang of the grapefruit complements the bland flavour and texture of the avocado. This is a very pretty individual salad, and a good accompaniment to a light baked fish.

½ pink grapefruit, peeled and cut into segments
1 small avocado, peeled and thinly sliced
15 ml (1 tablespoon) olive oil
10 ml (2 teaspoons) cider vinegar
pinch sugar
salt and pepper
1 head chicory leaves, separated
watercress, to garnish

DRAIN the juices from the grapefruit into a small bowl. Add the avocado slices and toss well. Arrange a row of avocado slices along the centre of a serving dish. In the same bowl beat together with a fork the oil, vinegar, sugar and seasonings. Arrange the grapefruit segments and chicory leaves around the avocado. Pour the dressing over the salad and garnish with the watercress.

Castle Fraser

CASTLE FRASER, to the west of Aberdeen, is the largest of the Castles of Mar. Someone called architecture 'music frozen in time'; if so, then Castle Fraser might be called a symphony. The castle was begun by Michael Fraser and largely finished by 1640. However, the charter of the original house dates from 1454.

Of the many Lairds of Castle Fraser, two characters stand out vividly. The first is the eighteenth-century Miss Elyza whose portrait hangs in the Worked Room. The room is so called because her abundant needlework, such as bed hangings and curtains, accomplished as she lay bedridden during her last years, is still in use.

The second vivid character is that of Charles Mackenzie Fraser who fought with Wellington in the Peninsular War in Spain, was wounded twice at the siege of Burgos in 1812, eventually losing a leg. Mementoes of this time are in the Library and include his bullet-holed hat and wooden leg in its carrying case. The fact that his leg was amputated did not prevent him from looking after and improving his estate and castle.

Charles's marriage to Miss Jane Hay resulted in a merry houseful of fourteen children. They created between them a home of many interests and made it a centre of hospitality and liveliness. One can imagine them raising their glasses in the old Scots toast, 'To food, fire and friendship'.

In 1921 the estate and castle became the property of the Pearson family, who began the restoration of the building. In 1946 Mr Pearson gave the castle to his daughter Lavinia who, with her husband Major Michael Smiley, continued the work before presenting the castle to the National Trust for Scotland in 1976. The old kitchen, which is now one of the Trust's tea-rooms, is particularly appreciated by visitors.

(Location: Off B993, 16 m W of Aberdeen, Gordon, Grampian.)

Fennel and Courgette with Yoghurt Dressing

Fennel and courgettes are popular vegetables which here make an unusual combination, well complemented by the tangy dressing.

salt
225 g (8 oz) courgettes, cut into
    thin sticks
1 bulb of fennel

Dressing
150 ml (¼ pint) natural yoghurt
15 ml (1 tablespoon) single cream
1 5 ml spoon (1 teaspoon) grain
    mustard

SPRINKLE some salt on the courgettes and leave to stand for 10 minutes to draw out excess moisture. Drain well, rinse with cold water, and dry on kitchen paper. Grate the fennel into a bowl, reserving the feathery tops, and add the courgettes. Put the yoghurt into a bowl and thin it with the cream. Add the mustard, mix well, taste for seasoning, then pour over the vegetables. Garnish with the feathery leaves of fennel.

Honey Lemon Dressing

This is a Mediterranean dressing which does not spoil and which prevents fresh fruits, particularly avocados, from turning brown.

175 g (6 oz) honey
125 ml (4 fl oz) lemon juice

½ 5 ml spoon (½ teaspoon)
    paprika pepper
pinch sea salt

COMBINE all the ingredients in a blender and mix at low speed until smooth. Store in a fridge. Use as a dressing for a green salad or fresh fruit or serve with cottage cheese.

Leek and Walnut Vinaigrette

Market gardens began to be cultivated near Edinburgh in the eighteenth century and the area around Musselburgh still maintains its reputation for growing fine leeks, the seed of which is greatly sought after by horticulturalists. Young leeks are best for salad and the older ones can be used for soups.

2 large leeks, washed and trimmed
25 g (1 oz) walnuts, chopped

Dressing
45 ml (3 tablespoons) oil
15 ml (1 tablespoon) wine vinegar
a pinch of caster sugar
½ 5 ml spoon (½ teaspoon) made
 mustard, either French or
 English
salt and pepper

CUT the leeks into 1 cm (½ in) pieces and shred some of the finest green part. Lay the shredded leek aside and blanch the rest of the leeks in boiling water for 2 minutes. Drain and cool. Put the leeks and walnuts into a bowl. In a large screw-top jar or a blender combine all the dressing ingredients. Taste for seasoning and pour over the leeks. Sprinkle with the reserved green part of the leeks and chill slightly before serving.

Mushroom Salad

For a tasty variation, try using raw mushrooms, sliced thinly, rather than cooked.

225 g (8 oz) mushrooms
a knob of butter
2 15 ml spoons (2 tablespoons)
 shredded celery
2 15 ml spoons (2 tablespoons)
 mayonnaise

1 crisp lettuce
1 hard-boiled egg, sliced, to
 garnish
1 beetroot, cooked, to garnish

SLICE and gently fry the mushrooms in butter. Leave to cool. Mix with the shredded celery then stir in the mayonnaise and pile the mixture on to a bed of lettuce. Garnish with sliced egg and beetroot.

Orange and Date Salad

Any fine salad oil such as olive, walnut or sesame should be used. Fresh dates are best in this salad and the sharp orange taste contrasts well with the sweetness of the dates.

125 g (4 oz) dates
45 ml (3 tablespoons) salad oil
salt
15 ml (1 tablespoon) lemon juice

2 sweet oranges
1 lettuce
1 15 ml spoon (1 tablespoon)
  walnuts, chopped

SOAK the dates in boiling water for a few minutes, then drain and wipe them dry. When cold, remove the stones and cut the dates into thin slices. Take the finest salad oil and pour it over the dates, sprinkle a little salt over, then add the lemon juice and mix well together. Peel the oranges and remove all white pith, then cut them into very thin slices and remove the seeds. Mix the oranges with the dates and arrange neatly on small lettuce leaves, sprinkling the chopped nuts over.

Pineapple and Pepper Salad

The pineapple was the ancient sign of hospitality in Scotland. A great stone pineapple forty-five feet high may be seen seven miles east of Stirling, built in 1761 as a garden retreat. The Trust hopes to restore the garden and woodland.

450 g (1 lb) tinned pineapple
  pieces
French dressing
1 green pepper, sliced finely

¼ cucumber, diced
50 g (2 oz) sultanas
1 lettuce, chopped

DRAIN the juice from the pineapple and combine with the French dressing. Mix all the remaining ingredients together in a bowl. Pour over the dressing and toss thoroughly.

Remoulade Sauce

A classic French sauce suitable for serving with a wide variety of cold foods.

a few leaves each of tarragon,
    burnet, chives, and parsley
1 egg yolk
salt and pepper
300 ml (½ pint) salad oil

15 ml (1 tablespoon) tarragon
    vinegar
1 5 ml spoon (1 teaspoon) made
    mustard
a pinch of caster sugar

BLANCH the herbs for 1 minute in boiling water, then dry well and chop them finely. Put the egg yolk into a small bowl, add salt and pepper, stir until very thick, then work in the oil, drop by drop at first, then more quickly. Add the vinegar, a few drops at a time, during the mixing, then add the mustard, herbs and sugar.

Special Green Salad

This salad is universal in its appeal. It can accompany any dish and can be varied to suit the supplies available.

1 clove garlic
1 lettuce or selection of various
    lettuces now available e.g.
    iceberg, cos, Webb, rosso, curly
    endive, oak leaf
½ small cucumber, cut in strips
1 carton cress
4 spring onions, sliced
½ green pepper, cut into strips
1 bunch watercress

Dressing
90 ml (6 tablespoons) olive or
    salad oil
½ 5 ml spoon (½ teaspoon) made
    mustard
30 ml (2 tablespoons) wine
    vinegar
a pinch of caster sugar
4 5ml spoons (4 teaspoons) capers,
    chopped
3 15 ml spoons (3 tablespoons)
    parsley, chopped

MAKE up the dressing by placing all the ingredients in a large screw-top jar and shaking well. Rub the garlic round the salad bowl and tear up the lettuces roughly. Place in the salad bowl with the cucumber, cress, onions and green pepper. Break up the watercress and add. Toss with the dressing just before serving or serve the dressing separately.

Timbale of Mushrooms

This recipe can be made with other vegetables such as courgettes or spinach and makes a splendid starter to a meal.

Serves 6–8

250 ml (9 fl oz) chicken stock
125 ml (4 fl oz) whipping cream
4 eggs
salt and pepper
a pinch of nutmeg
2 15 ml spoons (2 tablespoons)
   butter

225 g (8 oz) mushrooms, finely
   chopped
2 5 ml spoons (2 teaspoons)
   parsley
a pinch of tarragon

PLACE the stock, cream, eggs, salt and pepper and nutmeg in a bowl. Whisk until well blended. Melt the butter in a frying pan, add the mushrooms and stir over a high heat until lightly browned and dry. Add, with the parsley and tarragon, to the egg mixture. Pour into individual buttered moulds and set in a pan of water 2.5 cm (1 in) deep. Bake in a moderate oven, 180°C, 350°F, Gas Mark 4 for 30–35 minutes or until a knife inserted in the centre comes out clean. Serve hot, accompanied by fingers of toasted brown bread.

Threave Garden

SET IN GLORIOUS countryside in the south-west of Scotland, Threave is, foremost, an estate comprising farming, forestry, wildlife and a superb garden. In this lies much of its special attraction for visitors. From the beginning of the National Trust for Scotland's administration of Threave in 1948, it was felt that some specific purpose should be pursued, and so in 1960 the Threave School of Horticulture was established.

Through the activities of the students and the Trust's resident staff, over the years about sixty acres have been developed and transformed into not one but a multitude of gardens, each illustrating the full range of what can be achieved in a Scottish climate.

Students who go to Threave for a two-year course will already have had practical horticultural experience. One of the special advantages of Threave is the scope allowed for change: design of beds and walks can be readily altered and renewed, giving rare opportunities to students to put their own burgeoning ideas and skills into practice.

Most of the produce grown by the students is used in their hostel, Threave House, and the surplus is sold in the Threave shop. All aspects of gardening are studied: botany, genetics, soil science and the whole history of gardening.

A strong link exists with the Longwood Garden in Pennsylvania and an annual exchange of students is arranged. This is funded by the Scottish Heritage USA Inc (SHUSA), and to commemorate this the Longwood Steps in the Rose Garden were dedicated on the tenth anniversary of the scheme.

(Location: On A75, 1 m W of Castle Douglas, Dumfries and Galloway.)

Winter Brioche

Many shops now have patisserie departments selling all kinds of continental breads but if brioche is not easily obtained any large round continental bread would do.

Serves 4

1 very large brioche
225 g (8 oz) each baby carrots,
  turnips, parsnips, cauliflower
  mange-tout and button sprouts

50 g (2 oz) melted butter
salt and pepper

FIRST, cut a lid from the brioche. Remove the inside, leaving a 1 cm (½ in) lining. Prepare and cook all the vegetables separately until just tender, plunging each of them into cold water when cooked to preserve the colour. Drain and toss the vegetables together in melted butter. Season and arrange in the hollowed-out brioche. Replace the lid and cover with foil. Reheat at 180°C, 350°F, Gas Mark 4 for 15–20 minutes or until hot. Serve at once.

DESSERTS AND KICKSHAWS

Cooking is like love. It should be entered into with abandon or not at all.
VOGUE, Harriet Van Horne, 1956

AT one time the dessert, or kickshaw, at a Scots dinner was not served as a separate course on its own, as it is today, but it accompanied the meat or fish. 'Kickshaw' is a corruption of the French *quelque chose*. The word 'dessert' simply means 'the cloth removed' from the French word *desservir* meaning 'to clear the table', therefore dessert is that which comes after the cloth is removed.

Pastry of all kinds was much in evidence and still is. Many of the fruit-based puddings were served in pastry cases. Tall elegant glasses held syllabubs and flummeries, and the small glasses held delicate custards. One kind of Scots flummery was concocted from whipped cream, sugar, wine and nutmeg, all mixed together, put into glasses and sprinkled with toasted oatmeal.

Today the dining-room setting of the Georgian House in Charlotte Square, Edinburgh, with its silver, glass and fine china, recalls the age of elegance achieved in its Robert Adam design, while in the basement the kitchen, with its polished lines of copper jelly moulds and pans, reminds us of the life below stairs which was so much a feature of the great houses.

Priorwood Garden

THE MAJESTIC RUINS of Melrose Abbey rise beside the River Tweed, and nearby loom the Eildon Hills. Surely a rich enough heritage, but there is more. Lying behind a high red sandstone wall next to the abbey is an eighteenth-century house, now the Trust's shop and Visitor Centre for Melrose and the surrounding area.

The house itself is charming, but there is still more–a garden and a unique orchard. In medieval days the Cistercian monks of Melrose were skilled cultivators of the fine red earth of the land surrounding the abbey. They were also travellers and brought back from expeditions abroad a knowledge and appreciation of good husbandry. This of course included knowledge of the types of fruit, especially the apple, suitable for cultivation in the Borders.

Most Scottish children used to know the first lines of Sir Walter Scott's 'Lay of the Last Minstrel' which began: 'If thou shouldst view fair Melrose aright, go visit it by the pale moonlight'. In Scott's day, the custodian of the abbey was a man by the name of Bower who would conduct visitors around the building. The better to see the ruins, he would fix a candle on to a long pole saying, 'It disnae licht up the Abbey a' at yince but the lang can'le has this advantage ower the mune, that ye can see the ruins bit by bit that the mune canna and winna dae, inconstant cutty that she is.' (The word 'cutty' means a worthless lassie.)

An imaginative plan, formulated by Lady Bettina Thomson in the 1970s and now in successful operation, was to restore the Priorwood Garden and to establish a heritage orchard of many kinds of fruit. An 'Apple Walk' illustrates the history and development of the apple. A special feature is the area where flowers are grown, harvested and dried to make dried-flower arrangements which may be purchased.

(Location: Off A6091, in Melrose, Borders Region.)

Apple Amber

If you want to know the name of the man you will marry, peel the apple in one piece, throw the peel over your shoulder and it will fall in the shape of the first letter of your lover's name. So it is said!

Serves 6–8

4 large apples, peeled, chopped
   and cooked
3 eggs, separated

50g (2 oz) butter
150 g (5 oz) sugar
1 lemon

STRAIN the cooked apples or liquidize, and put into a greased pie dish. Beat the yolks of the eggs and blend with the butter into the apples with 50 g (2 oz) of the sugar. Add the lemon rind and juice. Whisk the egg whites very stiffly, fold in the remaining sugar and pile on top of the apple mixture. Bake in the oven at 190°C, 375°F, Gas Mark 5, until the meringue top is lightly browned.

Apple Mint Sorbet

One of the best known apples in Scotland was the Arbroath 'ozlin' which was brought to Scotland by the monks from their travels on the Continent.

Serves 4–6

450 g (1 lb) dessert apples
300 ml (½ pint) water
125 g (4 oz) granulated sugar
90 ml (6 tablespoons) white wine

4 15 ml spoons (4 tablespoons)
   sweet mint jelly
2 egg whites
apple slices, to garnish

WASH and roughly chop up the apples. Put in a saucepan with the water and sugar and simmer, covered, for 20 minutes, until soft. Press through a sieve. Stir the white wine and mint jelly into the warm apple purée and leave to go cold. Put in a rigid container and freeze until slushy. Whisk the egg whites until stiff and stir into the apple mint purée. Return to the freezer until solid. Serve in scoops with slices of fresh apple to decorate, or in biscuit flowers (see page 64).

Biscuit Flowers

These delicate biscuits make perfect dessert 'dishes' for sorbets, ices or soufflés.

Makes 10–12

75 g (3 oz) butter
100 g (3½ oz) vanilla sugar
1 egg

2 egg whites
125 g (4 oz) plain flour

CREAM the butter and sugar and add the eggs and flour until the mixture is smooth and thick. Cut 5-inch-diameter circles on greaseproof paper and lay on a baking tray or trays. Brush lightly with oil. Place a large teaspoonful of the mixture on each circle and bake for 20 minutes at 150°C, 300°F, Gas Mark 2. Take care the biscuits do not over-brown if the oven is too hot. Put a large mug or jar upside down on the table and oil it. This acts as the mould for the biscuits. Remove the tin from the oven and put one of the biscuits quickly on to the mould, pressing gently on top of a cloth. The edges cool into the shape of a wavy-edged flower. Take care to remove one biscuit at a time from the oven. If possible, have a row of upturned mugs or cups ready to hold the completed biscuit. Store in an airtight tin.

Bramble Snow with Almond Sauce

*Brambles in Scotland are called blackberries in England and in France they
are* mûres sauvages.

Serves 4–6

2 large cooking apples
450 g (1 lb) brambles
125 g (4 oz) caster sugar
50 g (2 oz) gelatine
2 egg whites

Almond Sauce
75 g (3 oz) ground almonds
3 drops almond essence
600 ml (1 pint) milk
2 5 ml spoons (2 teaspoons) plain
   flour
50 g (2 oz) caster sugar
2 egg yolks

CUT up the apples and put in a pan with the brambles and sugar. Cook gently
until soft, then strain and cool. Melt the gelatine in a little of the warmed
juice. Whisk the egg whites very stiffly, then add the purée of apples and
brambles, with the melted gelatine. Pour into a glass dish and leave to set. To
make the sauce, put the ground almonds and the essence into a saucepan with
half the milk and bring gently to the boil. Keep the pan over very low heat for
15 minutes. Strain off the milk, leaving the almonds as dry as possible.
Remove the almonds and pour the almond-flavoured milk back into the
saucepan. Mix the flour with the remaining milk, add to the pan and add the
sugar. Stir until boiling and boil gently for a few minutes. Whisk the egg
yolks and add to the mixture but do not boil. Allow to cool.

Cortachy Trifle

Central Scotland is excellent soft fruit country. Generations of youngsters make their summer pocket money by 'gae'n tae the berries', meaning 'going to the berry picking'.

Serves 6–8

3 eggs, separated
125 g (4 oz) caster sugar
125 g (4 oz) flour

450 g (1 lb) fresh raspberries
whisky
double cream, whipped

FIRST make the sponge. Beat the egg whites until very stiff, add the yolks and continue beating until pale brown in colour. Add half the sugar and beat again. Add the sieved flour and fold gently into the mixture, do not beat. Add 15 ml (1 tablespoon) boiling water. Pour into a straight-sided 15–20 cm (6–8 in) ovenproof dish and bake for 10 minutes at 220°C, 425°F, Gas Mark 7. Set aside a few raspberries for decoration. Sprinkle the remainder lavishly with sugar and allow to stand until the sugar has blended with the raspberries. Break down with a fork until mushy. Put the sponge into a dish the same size as the sponge itself, and sprinkle with a little whisky. Spoon the raspberry mixture on to the sponge and spread the whipped cream over. Decorate with the reserved raspberries.

Ellie's Muffin Pudding

In these days of more sophisticated eating, 'steam puds' do not figure quite so prominently, but they are nourishing and economical.

Serves 6

225 g (8 oz) stoned muscatel
  raisins
4 or 5 slices buttered bread
75 g (3 oz) sugar

coconut (optional)
1 egg
150 ml (¼ pint) milk

LINE a well-buttered pudding basin with the raisins. Fill the basin with alternate slices of the bread cut into small pieces to fit neatly, and a liberal sprinkling of sugar. A slight sprinkling of coconut may be added if liked. Make a custard with the egg and milk. Pour over the contents of the basin. Place a buttered paper and a clean cover cloth on top and steam for 2 hours.

Grosset Pie

Grosset is the Scots version of the French word for gooseberry, the groseille
à maquereau.

Serves 6–8

125 g (4 oz) butter	1 egg
125 g (4 oz) plain flour	1 egg yolk
50 g (2 oz) icing sugar	75 g (3 oz) caster sugar
a few drops vanilla essence	200 ml (7 fl oz) cream
350 g (12 oz) gooseberries	

RUB the butter into the flour and icing sugar until the mixture is crumbly, resembling breadcrumbs. Add the vanilla essence. Press the pastry into a flan dish and leave in a cool place for 1 hour if possible. Bake blind in a moderate oven, 180°C, 350°F, Gas Mark 4 for 30–40 minutes until brown all over (i.e. cover the centre with foil and fill with dried peas or beans). Sprinkle the gooseberries over the pastry. Whisk the egg, along with the separate egg yolk, sugar and cream and pour over the gooseberries. Bake in a moderate oven, 180°C, 350°F, Gas Mark 4, for about 30 minutes.

Orange and Raisin Topsyturvy Pudding

Topsyturvy means upside down; the Scots word is 'tapsalteerie'.

Serves 6

Base	Filling
2 oranges	50 g (2 oz) California raisins
30 ml (2 tablespoons) orange juice	125 g (4 oz) soft butter or
25 g (1 oz) butter	margarine
25 g (1 oz) light brown sugar	125 g (4 oz) light brown sugar
25 g (1 oz) California raisins	2 eggs
	175 g (6 oz) self-raising
	wholewheat flour
	1 5 ml spoon (1 teaspoon) baking
	powder
	60 ml (4 tablespoons) milk

REMOVE all peel and white pith from the oranges. Cut into thin slices. Heat together the orange juice, butter and sugar until the sugar has dissolved. Pour into a greased 20 cm (8 in) cake tin and arrange the orange slices on top. Sprinkle with raisins. Place the remaining raisins in a mixing bowl with all the pudding ingredients. Beat for 2–3 minutes until well mixed. Spoon the pudding mixture carefully over the base and smooth the top. Bake at 180°C, 350°F, Gas Mark 4 for 45 minutes, until firm to touch. Cool in the tin for 5 minutes, then turn out and cool on a wire rack.

Prune Mousse

An old-fashioned sweet seldom seen nowadays which makes unusual use of prunes.

Serves 4–6

225 g (8 oz) prunes, soaked
   overnight in enough red wine
   to cover
pared rind of ½ lemon
1 15 ml spoon (1 tablespoon)
   sugar, or less

2 5 ml spoons (2 teaspoons)
   gelatine
a dash of lemon juice, if liked
1 egg white, stiffly beaten
whipped cream and flaked
   almonds, to decorate

SIMMER the prunes in the red wine in which they were soaked, adding lemon rind and sugar to taste. When cooked, drain and stone, reserving the liquid. Liquidize or rub through sieve. Dissolve the gelatine in the prune juice over a gentle heat. Stir into the purée, with a little more sugar or a squeeze of lemon juice. When it is on the point of setting, fold in the egg white, and spoon into individual dishes. When set, decorate with whipped cream and almonds.

Ratafia Delight

A ratafia is a small biscuit or cake made of almonds.

Serves 4–6

225 g (8 oz) leftover sponge cake
8 ratafia biscuits
25 g (1 oz) glacé cherries
2 eggs

1 egg yolk
25 g (1 oz) caster sugar
300 ml (½ pint) milk, or more if
   required

BREAK the sponge into small pieces. Crumble the ratafias and add to the cake crumbs. Chop the cherries and put into a buttered mould. Fill the mould with the crumbs. Whisk the eggs and the egg yolk with the sugar, then stir in the milk. Pour over the cake and allow to stand for 30 minutes. Cover, then steam slowly for 30–45 minutes till the pudding is set. Remove from the saucepan and allow to stand for a minute or two and turn out gently on to a dish. Serve with whipped cream.

Note: This pudding may also be baked in the oven, with the mould standing in a baking tin containing hot water.

Greenbank Garden

THE SECOND HALF of the eighteenth century was a time when successful trading made rich men of many Glasgow merchants. In 1763 Greenbank House (not open to the public) was built for just such a merchant—one Robert Allason. At the same time, he had a walled garden constructed with an intricate lay-out. Substantial changes were made to the garden between then and 1976 when the Trust became the owners.

Over 200 years after the creation of Greenbank, when Glasgow is again thriving and full of visitors, the peace of the two-and-a-half-acre garden, as well as the twelve acres of policies, provide an added attraction for visitors.

Greenbank's attractive garden indicates how wide a range of ornamental plants, annuals and perennials, shrubs and trees can be grown in a relatively small area. Plants may be purchased and there is also a Gardening Advice Centre which is especially suitable for owners of small gardens. An unusual feature is the separate garden for the disabled, complete with special greenhouse and gardening tools.

(Location: Off A726, 6 m south of Glasgow city centre, in Clarkston, Eastwood District.)

Whim-Wham

Whim-Wham, which means something light and fanciful, is mentioned in Sir Walter Scott's The Bride of Lammermoor. *This recipe originated in the eighteenth century.*

Serves 6–8

25 g (1 oz) butter
50 g (2 oz) blanched almonds
25 g (1 oz) sugar
30 sponge fingers
150 ml (¼ pint) sweet sherry

50 ml (2 fl oz) brandy
finely grated rind and juice of
  1 large orange
300 ml (½ pint) double cream
275 g (10 oz) natural yoghurt

MELT the butter in a heavy pan and fry the almonds until golden brown. Stir in the sugar and cook for 1 minute, stirring well until the sugar is dissolved and the almonds coated. Tip on to a greased baking sheet and leave to cool. About 30 minutes before serving, break the sponge fingers in two and put in a bowl. Pour sherry, brandy, orange rind and juice over and leave to soak for 30 minutes. Whip the cream and fold in the yoghurt then spoon on to the sponges. Roughly chop the almonds and sprinkle on top. Serve immediately.

CAKE TIN

And had I but one penny in the whole wide world, Thou shouldst have it to buy gingerbread.

LOVE'S LABOUR'S LOST, William Shakespeare

IT has been said that 'every Scotswoman is born with a rolling pin under her arm'; be that as it may, there is no doubt that Scotswomen are famous for their baking. It was considered a 'terrible affront' if, when visitors called, the 'tins' were found to be empty.

A good baker has a certain prestige among her fellows and girls are taught at an early age to turn out the many delicacies which grace a Scots tea-table. In many old recipes an exceptionally large number of eggs seem to have been needed. This was because until the advent of baking powder in the nineteenth century, eggs were the chief raising agent.

It was Mary of Modena who first introduced tea to Scotland in 1618 and eventually it became popular. In the late nineteenth century an enterprising lady called Miss Cranston employed the then unknown architect Charles Rennie Mackintosh to design a tea-room in Sauchiehall Street, Glasgow. Emancipated ladies of the day ventured forth to take 'tea and cakes' with their friends—in public! The famous Scots tea-room grew, and many a juicy bit of gossip and confidence passed over the teacups. Mackintosh's later master-piece, the Hill House in Helensburgh, is now open to the public.

Tea is an important part of a visit to any Trust property and at most of the larger ones you can enjoy a 'cuppa' with good home baking and local jams in attractive surroundings, often in the kitchen or the servants' hall of the house.

Apple Cake

A good moist cake ideal for using up windfall apples. It is best kept in a cool place and eaten within a week. It is excellent for a packed lunch, spread with butter and eaten with a piece of mild Cheddar cheese.

350 g (12 oz) self-raising flour
½ 5 ml spoon (½ teaspoon)
  cinnamon
225 g (8 oz) margarine
175 g (6 oz) sugar
125 g (4 oz) sultanas

3 eggs
450 g (1 lb) cooking apples, peeled
  and cored
caster sugar and cinnamon to
  dredge

GREASE and line a 20 cm (8 in) cake tin. Sieve the flour and cinnamon and rub in the margarine. Add the sugar and sultanas. Beat the eggs well. Chop the apples roughly and stir into the mixture with the eggs. (No other liquid is required.) Place in the prepared tin and bake at 180°C, 350°F, Gas Mark 4 for 1–1¼ hours. Cool slightly in the tin then lift carefully on to a wire rack. Dredge with caster sugar mixed with a little more cinnamon. Serve spread with butter.

Haddo House

HADDO HOUSE, north of Aberdeen, was begun in 1732 for William Gordon, second Earl of Aberdeen, to a design by William Adam.

The Haddo Gordons were descended from the fifteenth-century de Gordon family. In the seventeenth century Sir John Gordon, a staunch royalist, was executed for his part in the Civil War. He is described as having been 'bold in all haserds, temperate in habit and kind to his subjects'. His son was made Lord High Chancellor of Scotland in 1682 and created the first Earl of Aberdeen.

The fourth Earl was brought up in London society, befriended specially by Henry Dundas and Prime Minister Pitt. When he returned to Haddo, he had little in common with his neighbours, who looked askance on him. One old servant remarked that he would have been a fine man 'gin they hadna' ta'en him to England and spoiled his education'. His long political career culminated in his post as Prime Minister from 1852 until 1855 in Queen Victoria's reign.

The sixth Earl left home to work incognito in Canada, then sailed to Australia as first mate on board the *Hera* but was washed overboard near Sable Island and drowned. The next Earl, his brother John, who later became the first Marquess of Aberdeen, married Ishbel Marjoribanks, daughter of Lord Tweedmouth. They had a long and happy life together, giving much to public service, the Earl serving both as Governor-General of Canada and Viceroy of Ireland.

The atmosphere today at Haddo still reflects the values of domestic and musical harmony, and perhaps, who knows, when a concert or play is in progress, echoes may waft to Philip Kemble, the actor friend of the fourth Earl, who often visited Haddo in times past. Today, the musical tradition is enhanced by the Haddo House Choral Society formed by David Gordon, the fourth Marquess and still energetically masterminded by his widow, June, Marchioness of Aberdeen.

(Location: Off B999, 19 m N of Aberdeen, Gordon, Grampian.)

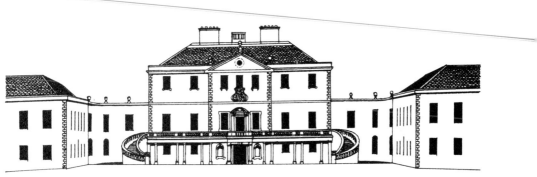

Canadian Fruit Tarts

A Christmas variation is to use 75 g (3 oz) currants, 25 g (1 oz) mixed candied peel and 10 ml (2 teaspoons) of sherry or brandy added to the egg. A delicious change from the usual mincemeat pies.

shortcrust pastry
25 g (1 oz) butter
125 g (4 oz) sugar

1 egg, well beaten
125 g (4 oz) currants

LINE 24 patty tins with shortcrust pastry. Melt the butter and sugar slowly, then remove from the heat. Cool slightly and mix in the beaten egg and currants. Allow to soak for about 10 minutes. Place a teaspoonful of the mixture in each pastry case and bake at 220°C, 425°F, Gas Mark 7 for 5 minutes, then reduce the heat to 200°C, 400°F, Gas Mark 6 for a further 15 minutes.

Crullas

The name comes from the Gaelic kril meaning a small cake or bannock. The Dutch krullen meaning 'to curl' is a similar type of cake and this may have been brought to Scotland by Dutch traders and settlers.

50 g (2 oz) butter
50 g (2 oz) caster sugar
2 eggs, beaten
275 g (10 oz) self-raising flour

oil or lard for deep frying
caster sugar, and carraway seeds
or cinnamon for dredging

CREAM the butter and sugar together and beat in the eggs thoroughly. Work in the flour to give a soft dough. Roll out and cut into long strips. Plait or twist two or three together and pinch the ends firmly. Fry in hot oil, drain well and dredge with flavoured sugar.

Fochabers Gingerbread

Gingerbread was originally a hard biscuit-type of cake but through the passage of time became the rich spicy cake which we enjoy today, cut thickly and spread with butter. It used to be stored in a wooden box with a tight-fitting lid.

50 g (2 oz) margarine
50 g (2 oz) lard
50 g (2 oz) caster sugar
125 g (4 oz) black treacle
1 size 2 egg, beaten
225 g (8 oz) plain flour
1 5 ml spoon (1 teaspoon) mixed spice
2 5 ml spoons (2 teaspoons) ground ginger

50 g (2 oz) ground almonds
50 g (2 oz) mixed peel
50 g (2 oz) currants
50 g (2 oz) sultanas
1 5 ml spoon (1 teaspoon) bicarbonate of soda
150 ml (¼ pint) beer

GREASE and line a 19 cm (7½ in) cake tin. Cream the margarine and lard and beat well. Beat in the sugar. Melt the treacle but do not allow to boil and add to the creamed mixture with the beaten egg. Sieve the flour with the spice and almonds and fold into the mixture. Fold in the dried fruit. Dissolve the bicarbonate of soda in the beer and beat into the mixture. Turn into the prepared tin, hollow the centre very slightly and bake at 150°C, 300°F, Gas Mark 2 for 1½–1¾ hours. Cool in the tin for 10–15 minutes before lifting on to a wire rack.

Fruit-filled Pancakes

These delicious pancakes make an up-to-date offering for a very special tea-party.

125 g (4 oz) flour
pinch of salt
25 g (1 oz) caster sugar
2 eggs plus 2 extra yolks
150 ml (¼ pint) milk
150 ml (¼ pint) cream
brandy
2 15 ml spoons (2 tablespoons)
   melted butter

Filling
25 g (1 oz) caster sugar
450 g (1 lb) redcurrants and
   loganberries mixed (or
   blaeberries and raspberries)
300 ml (½ pint) double cream
2 5 ml spoons (2 teaspoons) icing
   sugar
2 5 ml spoons (2 teaspoons)
   cinnamon, or 1 teaspoon
   ground cloves if preferred

Sieve the flour and pinch of salt into a basin and add the sugar. Put the eggs and the extra yolks into a well made in the dry ingredients and mix all together. Add the milk and cream gradually, and beat well until a smooth batter is made. Add enough brandy to make the batter thin. Put a little water and the sugar into a pan with the chosen berries and cook until the juices run. Sieve the berries or put through a blender (some people do not like the taste of the seeds of berries). Sweeten if desired. Whip the cream and flavour with the icing sugar and spice mixed together. Stir the melted butter into the batter mixture, and heat a small heavy frying pan until really hot, then lower the heat to medium. Brush the pan with a little extra butter and put in 2 tablespoonfuls of the batter, and cook until golden-coloured. Do not turn the pancake. Lift the pancake on to a warm plate and keep covered with foil in a warm oven. When all the batter is used, spread each pancake with 2 tablespoonfuls of the whipped cream and the berry purée, and fold over on to a warm serving plate.

Ginger Biscuits

A crisp, thinner version of the Ginger Snap, it is a popular biscuit at Hallowe'en and bonfire night. A tin of these spicy biscuits never lasts long if there are children in the house.

50 g (2 oz) lard
50 g (2 oz) margarine
2 5 ml spoons (2 teaspoons)
   golden syrup
175 g (6 oz) self-raising flour

75 g (3 oz) caster sugar
½ 5 ml spoon (½ teaspoon)
   bicarbonate of soda
1 5 ml spoon (1 teaspoon)
   ground ginger

MELT the fats and syrup in a pan but do not allow to boil. Add all the other ingredients, sieved together. Mix together well then remove from the heat. Form the mixture into small balls and place them well apart on a baking tray. Flatten slightly with the back of a fork. Bake at 190°C, 375°F, Gas Mark 5 for 10–15 minutes. Lift carefully on to a wire rack to cool.

Barrie's Birthplace

IN A LITTLE two-storey house in the small township of Kirriemuir set on a hillside in Angus, James Barrie, writer and playwright, was born in 1860. Kirriemuir's industry was handloom weaving, and was the source of much of Barrie's material for his plays and books.

He went to school first in Kirriemuir before moving to Dumfries where he attended the Academy. At Edinburgh University he gained his MA degree then worked as a journalist in Nottingham for eighteen months before going to live in London. He never forgot the pathos and humour of his native village and used them to illuminate his writings.

Barrie's passion for the theatre began at an early age. His first attempts at play-writing were staged behind his mother's house in Kirriemuir in a building that was really the communal wash-house. A model of the crocodile that for ever pursued Captain Hook in *Peter Pan* now lurks behind the outhouse door and generations of children still quake at the sight, and listen for the clock's tick.

The house is furnished with many of Barrie's own possessions—his desk, manuscripts, the warrant of the baronetcy conferred on him, his books and some of the costumes worn by different 'Peters' through the years.

When you have lingered in the birthplace, you can lift the latch of a door to enter a snug tea-room where the welcome is as warm as would have been that of Margaret Ogilvy, Barrie's mother.

(Location: A926 in Kirriemuir, 6 m NW of Forfar, Angus, Tayside.)

Kirriemuir Heckles

Angus bakers used a 'heckler'—a piece of wood with nails driven into it—to stamp out a pattern on the biscuits. This may be related to the heckler used for dressing the flax fibre for the linen industry which was an important domestic industry in Angus.

225 g (8 oz) softened butter or margarine
450 g (1 lb) self-raising flour
pinch salt

3 15 ml spoons (3 tablespoons) sugar
45 ml (3 tablespoons) water

RUB the margarine into the flour and salt. Melt the sugar in the water in a pan over a gentle heat until dissolved. Stir into the flour mixture and mix well. Roll into small balls and place on a greased baking tin. Flatten well and mark a circle of holes with a fork. Bake at 180°C, 350°F, Gas Mark 4 for 15–20 minutes.

Luscious Lemon Cake

A delicately flavoured sponge-type cake which is best eaten within a few days as the syrup makes it moist. It can be made as an orange cake if liked. It freezes well if cut into thick slices first and packed in foil or freezer wrap.

125 g (4 oz) butter
175 g (6 oz) caster sugar
175 g (6 oz) self-raising flour
60 ml (4 tablespoons) milk
2 large (size 2) eggs
grated rind of 1 large lemon

Syrup
3 15 ml spoons (3 tablespoons) icing sugar
45 ml (3 tablespoons) lemon juice

LINE the base of a 900 g (2 lb) loaf tin with greased paper. Put all the cake ingredients in a large bowl and beat with an electric whisk for 3–4 minutes until smooth and creamy. (It will take slightly longer if beating by hand.) Put into the tin and bake at 180°C, 350°F, Gas Mark 4 for 45 minutes. Leave in the tin to cool. Meanwhile, put the icing sugar and lemon juice in a small pan and bring to the boil. Pierce the cake all over with a skewer and spoon over the hot syrup. Leave in the tin until cold then store in an airtight tin.

Oat Crunchies

These crisp biscuits are equally good if made with muesli instead of porage oats. They are fragile when taken from the oven so handle with care. For a change, the sides may be dipped in melted chocolate.

125 g (4 oz) margarine
125 g (4 oz) caster sugar
1 5 ml spoon (1 teaspoon) each
 syrup and treacle
125 g (4 oz) self-raising flour
½ 5 ml spoon (½ teaspoon)
 bicarbonate of soda

5 ml (1 teaspoon) warm water
1 5 ml spoon (1 teaspoon) vanilla
 essence
75 g (3 oz) porage oats plus extra
 for rolling biscuits

CREAM the margarine and sugar and beat in the syrup and treacle. Sieve the flour and bicarbonate of soda and mix into the creamed mixture together with the water, vanilla and porage oats. Form into small balls and roll each in porage oats. Place well apart on a greased baking tin and bake at 180°C, 350°F, Gas Mark 4 for 10–12 minutes. Cool on a wire rack.

The Hill House

WE OWE A GREAT DEBT of gratitude to men of vision who sponsor men of genius. How fortunate, then, that Walter Blackie learned of the work of the Glasgow architect, Charles Rennie Mackintosh, from Talwin Morris, art director of Blackie's, his own publishing business. Blackie wanted a new house built for his family on a magnificent site high above Helensburgh on the hill overlooking the Clyde and chose Mackintosh as his architect.

The Hill House, while receiving the widest notice in the foreign press, was not the first impressive commission carried out by Mackintosh; he had already produced a masterpiece in the innovative building of the Glasgow School of Art in Renfrew Street, and also the tea-rooms for Miss Cranston in Sauchiehall Street, Glasgow. But long before that, Mackintosh had achieved much acclaim and the compliment of imitation by artists and designers on the Continent and in America. His reputation was particularly great in Vienna.

The Hill House had its interior design completed before its exterior, because Mackintosh wanted to create a house to service the lifestyle of the family and with furnishings and decoration blending into a complete entity. The elevations then followed. The apparent severe appearance somehow invites thoughts of a much earlier Scottish austerity, and yet is totally modern. The Trust is now restoring the garden to Charles Rennie Mackintosh's original designs.

Hill House came into the care of the National Trust for Scotland in 1982 through the financial assistance of the National Heritage Memorial Fund and with the approval of the Royal Incorporation of Architects in Scotland who had previously owned and maintained it.

(Location: Off B832, in Upper Colquhoun Street, Helensburgh, 23 m NW of Glasgow, Strathclyde.)

Paradise Cake

This is an excellent cake for a sales table at a fête as it cuts well in fingers.
As a variation the tin may be lined with shortcrust pastry and spread with
raspberry jam before adding the cake mixture.

125 g (4 oz) margarine
125 g (4 oz) caster sugar
2 eggs
50 g (2 oz) self-raising flour

50 g (2 oz) ground almonds
25 g (1 oz) raisins
25 g (1 oz) chopped glacé cherries
25 g (1 oz) sultanas

CREAM the margarine and sugar and beat in the eggs. Fold in the flour, ground almonds and fruit. Bake in a greased, base-lined Swiss roll tin at 190°C, 375°F, Gas Mark 5 for 25–30 minutes. Sprinkle with sugar while still warm.

Pitcaithly Bannock

A decorated cake of shortbread was the traditional bride's cake in some parts
of rural Scotland. It was known as an Infar Cake or Dreaming Bread
and was broken above the head of the bride as she entered her new home.
It was a token of goodwill and was intended to bring health and happiness to
the young couple. Portions of the cake were given to the young unmarried
girls to 'dream on'. The custom dates from Roman times when the sharing of
consecrated bread between consenting couples was recognized by law as a
binding contract of marriage!

175 g (6 oz) plain flour
25 g (1 oz) rice flour
75 g (3 oz) caster sugar
100 g (4 oz) butter, slightly
  softened

25 g (1 oz) candied mixed peel,
  chopped
25 g (1 oz) blanched almonds,
  finely chopped

SIEVE the flours and sugar together and work in the butter. Add the peel and almonds and form into a large round. Crimp the edges and place on a greased baking tray. Prick with a skewer right through to the tin. Mark in triangles and bake at 180°C, 350°F, Gas Mark 4 for 40 minutes. Halfway through the baking time re-mark the triangles. Cool on a wire tray and store in an airtight tin.

Scripture Cake

This cake is presented as a piece of history, a recipe that has been circulating for many generations. In 1968 it cost 7/10 or 40p!

1. 225 g (8 oz) Judges V: 25, last clause (butter)
2. 225g (8 oz) Jeremiah VI: 20 (sugar)
3. 1 15 ml spoon (1 tablespoon) I Samuel XIV: 25 (honey)
4. 3 Jeremiah XVII: 11 (eggs)
5. 225 g (8 oz) I Samuel XXX: 12, chopped (raisins)
6. 50 g (2 oz) Numbers XVII: 8, blanched (almonds)
7. 225 g (8 oz) Nahum III: 12 chopped (figs)
8. 450 g (1 lb) 1 Kings IV: 22 (flour)
9. Season II Chronicles IX: 9 (spices)
10. Pinch Leviticus II: 13 (salt)
11. 1 5 ml spoon (1 teaspoon) Amos IV: 5 (baking powder)
12. 45 ml (3 tablespoons) Judges IV: 19 (milk)

Beat numbers 1, 2, 3 to a cream. Add 4, one at a time. Add 5, 6, 7 and beat well. Add 8, 9, 10 and 11, having mixed them together. Lastly add 12. Put in a lined tin and bake in a slow oven at 150°C, 300°F, Gas Mark 2 for 1½ hours.

Simnel Cake

Simnel Cake for Lent was originally a light biscuit-type cake, boiled first and then baked. The name was transferred to a rich fruit cake in the seventeenth century.

125 g (4 oz) butter
125 g (4 oz) soft brown sugar
3 eggs, beaten
150 g (5 oz) plain flour
a pinch of salt
½ 5 ml spoon (½ teaspoon)
   ground mixed spice
350 g (12 oz) mixed currants,
   raisins and sultanas
50 g (2 oz) mixed peel

grated rind of ½ lemon
a little apricot jam
beaten egg, to glaze

Almond Paste
125 g (4 oz) ground almonds
125 g (4 oz) caster sugar
1 egg, beaten
½ 5 ml spoon (½ teaspoon)
   almond essence

MAKE the almond paste by mixing the ground almonds and sugar with enough beaten egg to give a fairly soft consistency. Add the essence and knead well till smooth and pliable. Roll out one-third to make a circle 18 cm (7 in) in diameter. Reserve the rest for the top of the cake. To make the cake, cream the butter and sugar and beat in the eggs. Add the flour, salt, mixed spice, dried fruit, peel and grated rind. Put half the mixture into a greased and lined 18 cm (7 in) cake tin. Smooth the top and add the circle of almond paste. Add the rest of the cake mixture and smooth the top, hollowing the centre slightly. Bake in a pre-heated oven at 140°C, 275°F, Gas Mark 1 for 1½–2 hours. When the cake is cold, brush the top with warm apricot jam. Form 11 small balls from the reserved almond paste and lay aside. Roll out the remainder to cover the top of the cake. Arrange the balls round the edges and brush with beaten egg. Bake in the oven at 180°C, 350°F, Gas Mark 4 till the almond paste has browned. If liked, the centre may be filled with small coloured Easter eggs. This cake keeps well in a tin for 2 weeks or more.

SWEETIE JAR

Finis
F for France and I for dance
N for nickety-boundie,
J for Jess, the printer's wife
And S for sugar candy.

FOR a long time, sugar came not in convenient paper bags but in a hard conical shape, from which pieces had to be hacked off with ferocious metal cutters. Examples of these cones can be seen today at the Georgian House in Charlotte Square, Edinburgh and at Brodick Castle on the Isle of Arran.

Scotland is infamous for her love of sweeties, from the soothing pandrop sucked surreptitiously in church to 'gob-stoppers', those marble-like bullets which afforded amazing changes of colour every 'sook', and could be swapped in school playgrounds for a go with the 'sherbet dab' or liquorice strap. What ancient joys!

In country places, the making of tablet and toffee was often the excuse for a bit of 'daffing' or courting, when conversation lozenges could be passed round (known as 'readin' sweeties') with their passionate messages in pink, green or blue, saying, 'Be my love' or 'Meet me tonight' or 'Be true to me'.

An old saying about the making of sweeties goes, 'You need a clear fire, a clean pan and a good-natured cook'.

Chocolate Walnuts

Walnuts came originally from Persia. The word walnut comes from the Anglo-Saxon word wealh, *meaning foreign or exotic. It is said that walnut trees thrive best if the nuts are beaten off with sticks and not gathered.*

15 g (½ oz) powdered gelatine
  (make according to instructions
  on the packet)
275 g (10 oz) sieved icing sugar
15 ml (1 tablespoon) cold water

25 g (1 oz) glucose
50 g (2 oz) powdered chocolate
few drops vanilla essence
225 g (8 oz) shelled walnuts

PUT the gelatine and half the sugar with the water into a pan and stir until it comes to the boil. Add the glucose and stir until thoroughly melted. Put the rest of the icing sugar on a work surface. Melt the chocolate in a double saucepan. Put the hot sugar mixture into the centre of the dry sugar, add to it the melted chocolate and vanilla essence, then work all to a smooth paste. Make the mixture into small balls. On each side of these press the halves of the walnuts, and put in a cool place to harden and to dry. When quite hard, arrange in a long box and store. (This is a good sweet to add to a gift box at Christmas.)

Ginger and Coconut Tablet

Ginger originates in south-east Asia and has been used in India and China since very ancient times. It had reached Britain and was in common usage by the eleventh century both in food and medicine.

350 ml (12 fl oz) cold water
1.75 kg (4 lb) soft brown sugar
  (not Demerara)
50 g (2 oz) butter

pinch of salt
225 g (8 oz) preserved ginger,
  minced
125 g (4 oz) dessicated coconut

BRING the water to the boil and dissolve the sugar in it. Add a large lump of butter and a pinch of salt. Stir while boiling until it begins to thicken. Add the ginger and the coconut. Beat with a large fork for several minutes until it begins to set as tablet. Pour into buttered tins and cut with a knife before it gets quite cool.

Glessie

The word glessie describes the glass-like quality of this sweet. Modern chefs use it to spin gossamer cobwebs over special desserts, but it is not new, being made by seventeenth-century hostesses as embellishment.

30 ml (2 tablespoons) water
1 5 ml spoon (1 teaspoon) cream
  of tartar

250 g (½ lb) soft sugar
25 g (1 oz) butter
750 g (1½ lb) golden syrup

USE an enamelled pan. Put the water, cream of tartar, sugar and butter into the pan and bring slowly to the boil. Boil for 5 minutes. Add the syrup and boil for a further 30 minutes. Pour out thinly into very well buttered tins and allow to cool. Cut into sticks.

Gundy

Gundy is a traditional Scottish sweet, but the word also means a push or shove. A gundyman was not only a seller of sweets—there is another meaning. A gundyman was a ploughman's assistant who operated the long pole fastened to the ploughbeam, pushing or pulling the plough as occasion required.

450 g (1 lb) brown sugar
1 5 ml spoon (1 teaspoon) syrup
 or black treacle

50 g (2 oz) butter
pinch of cinnamon or aniseed

PUT all the ingredients into a pan, and bring gently and slowly to the boil. Continue boiling 'to the crack': that is until it becomes quite hard when a little is put into cold water. Flavour with aniseed or cinnamon. Pour out very thinly on a buttered tin or slab, and when it is cold and hard, break it up roughly with a small hammer wrapped in muslin cloth.

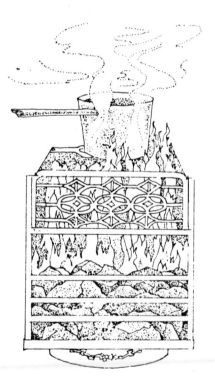

The Weaver's Cottage

THIS IS A TYPICAL cottage of an eighteenth-century handloom weaver. It was built in 1723 by Andrew, John and Jenet Bryden whose names appear on the lintel over the front door.

The medieval families of Kilbarchan, a small village in Renfrewshire, made their living from farming; it was not until late in the seventeenth century, when the population had risen to almost 1000, that weaving was introduced. By the end of the nineteenth century it was the main industry. While neighbouring Paisley relied on the then current fashion for shawls to give them work, Kilbarchan weavers kept their options open and turned out many different kinds of cloths right into the 1950s.

Through the interest and generosity of local people, displayed in the cottage are many more examples of artefacts, tools, furnishings and bygones than might have existed in one weaver's cottage. One of the latest weavers of Kilbarchan was Willie Meikle, and his tools are to be seen, including his loom, reeds, shuttles and pirn-wheels. This wealth of material enables a change of display to be made from time to time. Box-beds were of course in common use and in one room a section of wall has been cut out to enable the occupant of the bed to stretch out. In another room there is a stone bed-head. The simple kitchen range with its girdle and open fire, with clothes drying in front of it, is a popular feature.

In the garden are various interesting stones and there is a bee-bole set in the wall to take three skips or bee-hives. Boles were originally small openings to allow air and light to penetrate a cupboard for holding odds and ends.

From time to time, there are demonstrations of weaving using the old looms.

(Location: Off A737, in Kilbarchan, 12 m SW of Glasgow, Strathclyde.)

Marzipan Dates in Caramel

Medieval cooks called marzipan 'marchpane'. The word originated in Italy, and was taken over by the Germans from whom marzipan was imported into this country.

225 g (8 oz) ground almonds
125 g (4 oz) caster sugar
125 g (4 oz) icing sugar
1 egg or 2 egg yolks
1 box dates

Caramel
450 g (1 lb) granulated sugar
150 ml (¼ pint) lemon juice
150 ml (¼ pint) water

To make the marzipan, mix the almonds, sugars and eggs together into a smooth paste. Remove the stones from the dates without cutting the fruit in two or breaking it. Fill the centres with pieces of marzipan shaped into almonds, and roll slightly with the hands to make a neat shape. Allow these to dry for a few hours. Make the caramel by putting the sugar, lemon juice and water into a heavy pan and boiling quickly until a golden brown colour. Remove the pan from the heat and dip the bottom of the pan into very cold water to prevent burning the caramel. Dip each date into the warm caramel and dry out on a wire tray. This last process must be accomplished very swiftly because the caramel hardens quickly, so four hands are better than two.

Nougat

Nougat used to be sold in thick rice paper, packed in boxes in which were tiny gold forks with which to choose the pieces of nougat.

450 g (1 lb) icing sugar
4 egg whites
125 g (4 oz) clear honey
75 g (3 oz) sweet almonds, shredded

1 15 ml spoon (1 tablespoon) pistachio nuts, shredded
50 g (2 oz) glacé cherries, finely chopped

Sieve the sugar and put it in a bowl with the whites of the eggs and the honey. Mix well and set the bowl over a pan of hot water, and continue to whisk the mixture until white and thick. This may take about 30 minutes. Keep the mixture away from the sides, mixing all the while. Remove from the pan, and add the nuts and the cherries. Line a baking tin with wafer paper, press the nougat down into the tin, cover with more wafer paper and put a weight on top. When cold, cut into small pieces with a very sharp knife, and wrap in wax paper.

Peppermint Creams

The making of peppermint creams is a fine occupation for children on a wet Saturday morning, and gives them a great sense of achievement!

1 egg white
450 g (1 lb) icing sugar
oil of peppermint or peppermint
  essence

a little green colouring (optional)
melted chocolate (optional)

BEAT the egg white till frothy but not stiff. Sieve the icing sugar and gradually work it into the egg white to give a firm paste. Add the peppermint to taste. (If liked, divide the mixture into two and add green colouring to one half, so giving a mixture of white and green sweets.) Knead it till smooth and roll out on a board dusted with icing sugar. Cut into small circles and leave to set overnight. For a professional touch, dip in melted chocolate.

Sponge Candy

Use a very large pan for this sweetmeat, as it puffs up. Do not allow children to make this unless properly supervised.

1 kg (2 lb) brown sugar
250 ml (9 fl oz) cold water

2 5 ml spoons (2 teaspoons)
  baking soda

PUT the sugar in a large pan with the water and boil for 20 minutes. Test in cold water and if it cracks, it is ready. Draw off the heat and add the baking soda. It will froth and puff up in the pan. Pour into a deep buttered tin and leave to cool. Cut into bars when cold.

Kellie Castle

PEOPLE BORN AND brought up in Fife are proud to say that they belong not to Fife, but to the 'Kingdom' of Fife. There was for a long time a continuity of trade between Scotland and the Low Countries, with a multitude of small ships sailing the uncertain waters of the North Sea. These commercial activities led, in time, to a high level of prosperity in the 'Kingdom'.

The first castle at Kellie, as we see it now, was of the kind known as a 'keep', built in 1360 for defence: tall, narrow and severe. Three other towers were added during the next 200 years and eventually, by the beginning of the seventeenth century, all the towers had been joined by various building operations including the erection of a great hall, 'spacious and new'.

The castle was the property of the Oliphant family from 1360 until 1613. It then passed to Viscount Fenton, later first Earl of Kellie, and remained in that family for many years. On the death of the tenth Earl in 1829, a 'muckle roup' of its contents was held and the castle virtually abandoned for the next forty-five years.

Then, by great good fortune, Professor James Allan Lorimer of Edinburgh, while on holiday in Fife, discovered the neglected building and took over the castle from the owner of the time, the Earl of Mar, as an 'improving tenant'. The Lorimer family took up residence there in 1878, but it was not until 1948, after great vicissitudes, that Kellie Castle at last actually belonged to the Lorimer family.

From time to time, in some of the great houses of Scotland, a particular personality seems to shine through, and so it is at Kellie Castle, where the talents and perception of Mary Lorimer, wife of Hew Lorimer the sculptor, transformed the rooms into places of 'firmness, commoditie and delight'.

(Location: Off A921 between Leven and Crail, Fife.)

Sugar Mice

Surely no Christmas stocking can be complete without its pink or white sugar mouse nestling in the toe!

900 g (2 lb) granulated sugar
400 ml (13 fl oz) water
½ 5 ml spoon (½ teaspoon)

cream of tartar (this prevents the sugar from crystallizing)
pieces of fine string for the tails

HEAT the sugar and water over a low heat and gradually bring to the boil. Stir till the sugar dissolves. Add the cream of tartar, cover and bring to the boil again. Heat to 115°C (240°F). If no thermometer is available, drop a small amount into icy water. If this forms a small ball which flattens when put on a plate, it is ready. Pour immediately on to a dampened marble slab or hard board. Leave to cool and stir with a wooden spatula or spoon until smooth. Divide and add colouring to each section if wished, or leave white. Stir each section in turn (if they have been coloured) until a lump has been formed. Mould into small roly-poly shapes with a sharp end for the head. Insert a piece of string for the tail, using a small skewer, then smoothing the join. Pinch out the ears, mark the mouth and indicate the eyes with a grain of chocolate, or a silvered sugar ball used for cake decoration.

Toffee Apples for Hallowe'en

Hallowe'en, even nowadays, is a time for gatherings of friends and children. In years past cattle and horses would be well locked up in the stable and byre, for it was well known that witches in particular would take away a good beast and ride it till the mane was all a-tangle and the horse be unfit for work the next day. Rowan berries and leaves were twined into little bunches and hung above stable doors, for no witch or goblin could pass a rowan unscathed. Dipping or 'dooking' for apples and roasting of nuts are survivals of rituals about the laying up of stores for winter, and the last sheaf of the harvest would, if possible, be kept till Christmas when it would be divided up among the cattle to make them thrive the following year.

8 eating apples
450 g (1 lb) brown sugar

150 ml (¼ pint) water
225 g (8 oz) golden syrup

WASH and dry the apples. Push a stick firmly into the end of each one. Grease a baking sheet. Put the sugar and water into the saucepan, and heat gently until the sugar is dissolved, stirring a little. Add the syrup. Boil to about 143°C (290°F). Remove the pan from the heat. Pour a little toffee into a bowl of cold water; if ready, it should be fairly brittle. Dip the apples one at a time into the toffee, twisting to make sure they are completely covered in toffee. Stand the apples on the baking tray, stick upwards. When hard and cool, wrap each in cellophane paper if not to be eaten at once.

Turkish Delight

This may be a complete misnomer in the same way as Turkey rhubarb has nothing to do with Turkey, nor did turkeys come from Turkey, so perhaps this sweetmeat needs a new name.

450 g (1 lb) sugar
25 g (1 oz) powdered gelatine
300 ml (½ pint) water
15 ml (1 tablespoon) lemon juice
15 ml (1 tablespoon) rose water
  (obtainable from chemists)

a few drops food colouring (pink or green)
1 15 ml spoon (1 tablespoon) cornflour
2 15 ml spoons (2 tablespoons) icing sugar

Mix the sugar and the gelatine well together and put into a medium-sized, heavy-based pan with the water. Melt over a gentle heat till clear and completely dissolved. Bring to the boil and boil for 5 minutes, stirring gently. Remove from the heat and stir in the lemon juice and rose water with a little food colouring. Allow to cool for a minute and then draw a piece of greaseproof paper over the surface to clear it. Pour into a 15 cm (6 in) oiled tin and leave overnight. Next day, mix the cornflour and icing sugar together and sprinkle over a work surface and dust a sharp knife with it. Carefully ease the mixture out of the tin and cut it in 6 strips, then cut each into 6 cubes. Toss these in the cornflour mixture and store in an airtight box or tin with a layer of cornflour mixture between each layer of sweetmeat. To serve after a meal, arrange on a plate with a container of cocktail sticks in the centre.

Note: Creme de Menthe may be used instead of rose water.

DAIRY

Many's the long night I've dreamed of cheese—toasted, mostly.

TREASURE ISLAND, R. L. Stevenson

ALTHOUGH south-west Scotland, with its famous herds of dairy cattle and lush pastureland, is a major cheese-making area, excellent cheeses are also made in other parts of Scotland.

Cheese-making was an essential part of the work of the housewife and dairy maid and played a vital role in the diet of the Scots people. It was an ideal way in which to preserve milk, a valuable protein, in the summer when it was both plentiful and of good quality for the lean days of winter. Bannocks, smoked or dried fish and cheese sustained many a Scot in times of hardship.

Until the seventeenth century skimmed milk was used for cheese-making, the cream being used to make butter. The use of full cream in cheese-making is attributed to a Barbara Gilmour who, on returning to her home in Ayrshire after a time spent in Ireland to escape the Covenanter troubles, brought with her a recipe for a full cream hard cheese from which developed the famous Dunlop cheese. The old custom of storing cheese in a barrel of oatmeal until it was required comes from Orkney.

After the Second World War farmhouse cheese-making declined; more cheese was made in commercial creameries. However, there has been a revival of this old skill in recent years and many interesting and tasty cheeses made from cow's, ewe's and goat's milk can be purchased in speciality cheese shops and delicatessens.

In 1983 the Company of Scottish Cheesemakers introduced the Scottish Cheese Mark. It is a round paper label with a blue centre circle and a blue wedge shape half in and half out of the circle with the words 'Scottish Cheese' above it. It will be found on the wrapper of all Scottish Cheddar and Dunlop cheese produced by registered users. Its purpose is to monitor and control quality and to give information to the customer.

Cheese is the ultimate quick food. It can be eaten at any meal, either raw or cooked. It makes an excellent ending to a meal as it was served in the great country and town houses in the last centuries. In many of the dining rooms of the National Trust properties wooden cheese coasters can be seen adorning the sideboards and cheese presses are on show at several houses, including House of Dun. Following the simplicity of Scottish cooking, cheese was usually eaten raw accompanied by oatcakes.

Some Scottish Cheeses

Barac: a hard cheese made from ewe's milk, it has a sharp taste with an 'after' bite.

Bonchester: a rich full cream soft cheese similar to Brie made from Jersey milk.

Caboc: known as the 'Chieftain's cheese' it is made from a fifteenth-century recipe from the West Highlands. It is a soft full cream cheese rolled in pinhead oatmeal.

Crowdie: a traditional cheese made from skimmed milk, it resembles a smooth cottage-type cheese. It was sometimes called the 'hangie' as the curds are suspended in a cheesecloth or muslin bag to drain.

Crowdie and Cream: a mixture of crowdie and double cream which is sold in cartons and can be used for cheesecake and desserts.

Dunlop: a more mellow cheese than Cheddar, softer and creamier in texture. Like Cheddar there are different types such as Arran and Islay.

Galic: a soft cream cheese flavoured with wild garlic and rolled in flaked nuts.

Gruth Dhu: a mixture of 2 parts crowdie and 1 part double cream rolled in crushed peppercorns.

Highland Choice: an Islay Dunlop flavoured with Drambuie and flaked almonds.

Highland Herb: Dunlop from Islay flavoured with chives and Scots mustard.

Hrasma: a soft cream cheese with a wild garlic flavour made from double cream and sold in cartons as a spreading cheese.

Lanark Blue: made from ewe's milk it is somewhat like Roquefort.

Langskail: a Gouda-type cheese made in 1 lb/450 g rounds with a distinctive red skin.

Lothian: a Camembert-type mature soft cheese with a white mould and distinctive flavour. It can be eaten while still firm or left till soft.

Orkney: similar to Dunlop but with a special flavour. Can be white, red or smoked in small individual rounds.

Peat Smoked: full fat soft cheese made in individual rounds on straw mats and smoked over peat to give a unique flavour.

Pentland: a Brie-type soft cheese which is very runny when ripe.

Scottish Cheddar: the favourite in Scottish households this is a firm-textured hard cheese, mild when young and maturing to a real 'bite'. It is mostly rindless and can be obtained red or white. There are various types of Cheddar such as Arran, Islay, Galloway and Orkney.

Stewart: mild tasty blue cheese similar to, but less strong than, Stilton.

PANTRY

A good housewife must be able to compound an elixir as well as a pudding.

WE forget how recent supermarkets are. The village shop, alas, is no longer to be found in every small community throughout Scotland. Not everyone has a car either. It is therefore as important as it certainly used to be, for each household to have a pantry. Farmhouses and country houses used to make and fashion their own stores of everyday items such as we now buy in shops. Bandages were made from torn strips of old sheets and furniture polish was made from the wax of the local bees. For 200 years there has existed a recipe for alleviating a sore throat which was certainly a favourite in Scottish farmhouses well into the 1930s. This was a cup of good thick blackcurrant jam, from the garden of course, mixed with thick cream, all stirred up together. A spoonful of this from time to time was guaranteed to banish the tickliest of coughs.

In well-appointed pantries could be found stores of honey, almonds, rose water, ginger, treacle, cinnamon, jams and jellies of every sort, colour and flavour. During the Second World War, precious tins of fruit were to be found which were obtained with an accumulation of 'points', with raisins and other dried fruits. 'Onion Johnnies' are now seldom seen, but in recent times past, most kitchen pantries had strings of good French onions hanging there.

Many of the old kitchen utensils, such as spice boxes, orange cutters and sugar scrapers, now long forgotten, can be found in the kitchens at Drum Castle, Aberdeenshire and at Brodie Castle in Morayshire.

Almond Brittle

Almonds have long been imported from the Middle East, and here make an irresistible topping for dessert or cake.

450 g (1 lb) sugar
300 ml (½ pint) water
125 g (4 oz) almonds

1 5 ml spoon (1 teaspoon) cream of tartar

MELT the sugar very slowly with the water in a shallow pan until it reaches a syrup-like consistency. Add the almonds, cream of tartar and stir quickly. Pour into a greased toffee tin and mark into squares immediately the top begins to set. These will break up easily when cold. Store in a jar with a tight-fitting lid.

Killiecrankie

IN 1947 FIFTY-FOUR acres of Perth and Kinross came into the care of the National Trust for Scotland at Killiecrankie, and in 1964 the Trust opened a purpose-built centre to explain to visitors the history of the famous battle.

In the long struggle between the Covenanters and the Catholics, John Graham of Claverhouse, Viscount Dundee, was an ardent royalist and most assiduous in hunting down the Covenanters. History has given him the gentle title of 'Bonnie Dundee', but he was also known as 'Bloody Clavers'.

There is a story told of the shooting of the 'Christian carrier', one John Brown of Ayr, a man of peace whose only fault was that he did not attend the parish church but worshipped in private. Claverhouse and his men surrounded Brown's house, ordering him to take the prescribed oath of allegiance to James II or face death. Brown preferred to follow his conscience, and in front of his wife and child he was shot dead. 'What do you think of your bonnie man now?' asked Claverhouse. The widow answered, 'I aye thocht muckle o' him, but never sae muckle as I do this day.'

It was at Killiecrankie in 1689 that the first shots were fired in the Jacobite cause. Claverhouse, leading his Highland army, marched on Blair Atholl, while General Hugh Mackay, at the head of the troops of King William, came up through the pass to confront the Jacobites. Mackay's force was routed, but in the moment of triumph Claverhouse himself was killed.

The rocks in the river below, where a government soldier jumped the river, fleeing from his pursuers, are still known as the Soldier's Leap.

(Location: On A9, 3m N of Pitlochry, Perthshire, Tayside Region.)

Apple and Ginger Jam

Jam or jelly is ready or 'set' when a spoonful is taken from the pan and allowed to cool for a few moments on a plate, then touched to see if a 'skin' forms.

3 kg (7 lb) apples
2.5 cm (1 in) piece of fresh root
  ginger, peeled

rind and juice of 3 lemons
1 litre (1¾ pints) water
2 kg (5 lb) sugar

PEEL, quarter and core the apples. Tie the apple peel, ginger and lemon rind in a muslin bag and add, with the apples, to a pan of water. Bring to the boil and simmer for 30 minutes or until soft. Remove the muslin bag, squeezing out as much juice as possible. Add the sugar and stir until dissolved. Stir in the lemon juice. Increase the heat and bring the jam to the boil. Boil for 15–20 minutes or until set point is reached. Skim off the scum from the surface and allow the jam to cool for 5 minutes. Pour into warmed jars and cover at once.

Beetroot Relish

The flavours of beetroot and vinegar marry well together, while the vinegar helps to soften the fibres of the beetroot.

1 kg (2 lb) beetroot
vinegar

1 packet of redcurrant jelly

WASH the beetroot well and boil until soft. Remove the skin and chop the beetroot into small pieces, then place in a dish and barely cover with vinegar. Melt the jelly in 300 ml (½ pint) water. Pour over the beetroot and allow to cool before putting in jars with close-fitting lids.

Pitmedden Garden

ABOVE THE ENTRANCE to the Great Garden of Pitmedden there is an inscription: FUNDAT 2 MAY 1675–SAS DML. Although the inscription is a reproduction, one can just imagine the stone-mason and his workmen nearing the end of their labours on a fine spring day in that corner of Aberdeenshire, not exactly known for its amiable climate. The 'win's are blawin' saft frae the west', curlews are wheeling in the clear cold air and the masons have just completed the initials of Sir Alexander Seton and his wife Dame Margaret Lauder, the owners of Pitmedden.

Sir Alexander and his brother were wards of their kinsman, the third Earl of Winton whose castle, near Tranent in East Lothian, was where they spent most of their boyhood. The Earl was involved in many building projects and this, no doubt, greatly influenced the two young boys. Sir Alexander became an advocate, a Senator of the College of Justice and Member of Parliament for Aberdeenshire in the Scottish Parliament. However, he opposed the measures to re-establish Catholicism which did not endear him to James II, and so he was forced to retire from public life to look after his estate at Pitmedden.

Gardens in ancient days existed as 'pleasances', where people enjoyed the out-of-doors, or as places for the growth of medicinal herbs. For greater convenience and compactness, these herbs were cultivated in precise areas specifically created for them. Much later, gardens 'in the grand manner', a competely new approach, were created by André Le Nôtre of Paris at Vaux-le-Vicomte and Versailles. Since the Scots were constant travellers to the Continent, Sir Alexander no doubt saw and heard of the new ideas and applied the parterre designs to his own garden at Pitmedden. Now, over 300 years later, the garden has been restored and is lovingly cared for by the National Trust for Scotland.

(Location: On A920, 14 m N of Aberdeen, Gordon, Grampian.)

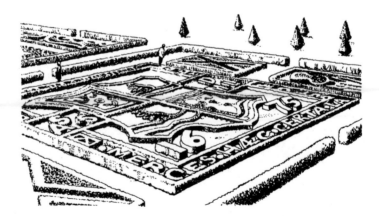

Bouquet Garni

Even if you have no back yard or garden you can still grow herbs in window boxes, roof gardens, balconies and patios. Not only do herbs provide healthy fresh green material, but they also look very attractive.

THIS usually consists of a bay leaf, parsley and thyme, tied together in sprigs in muslin or cheesecloth. All herbs should be dried in airy, shady places where there is no condensation. Dried herbs will keep for about a year, but if they have been finely powdered, they may lose their savour more quickly. Parsley and lemon balm keep for a shorter time than rosemary, basil, thyme or marjoram. Remember that a sprig of fresh parsley, if available, will bring out the flavour of the dried herbs.

Candied Orange Peel

Not so often found in household cupboards today, but very useful for decoration.

6 oranges   350 ml (12 fl oz) water
450 g (1 lb) sugar

REMOVE the orange skins in halves if possible. Scrape away all the white pith. Soak the skins in slightly salted water for 3 or 4 days. Drain on a cloth, then boil in plenty of water until quite soft. Drain well on a sieve and put into a basin. Boil the sugar and a cupful of water for about 10 minutes to make the syrup. Pour over the peel. Cover the basin and leave for several days. Pour off the syrup into a saucepan, bring to the boil and add the peel. Boil until it is clear and until very little syrup is left in the pan—this may take 15 minutes. Spread the peel on to a greased dish, put a little syrup into the hollows of the peel and dust with sugar. Set in a warm place to dry and candy. Store in a jar with a close-fitting lid.

Brodie Castle

THERE HAVE BEEN Brodies at the lands of Brodie beside the Moray Firth for over 800 years – some 400 years before the present castle was built. The present Brodie – the twenty-fifth – lives in a private wing of the castle and often delights visitors by standing in as an incognito guide. He derives great pleasure from showing visitors his family treasures of fine French furniture, superb porcelain and a major collection of paintings.

One small girl and her companion who visited the castle on an August day of gentle sunshine were immediately enchanted by the play area, thoughtfully established between the car park and the castle.

Then, being a junior member of the National Trust for Scotland, the girl presented her membership card at the entrance to the castle. Standing in the hall was Brodie of Brodie himself, who came forward welcomingly. The little girl politely stretched out a small hand which the Laird took in his. It was a charming introduction for her to what might well become a lifetime's association with the Trust.

It was interesting to see a great property through the eyes of the child. She was cast down at there not being a copy of *Puff the Magic Dragon* in the library and the portraits evinced some acute comment, but it was inevitably the nursery that took her heart. There the two small 'tower' areas are filled with magic: old books, old games and puzzles; the toy prams of generations of small people; dolls with trousseaux, but best of all, and waiting for who knows what adventures in the future, were the rocking horses.

This visit, which that small girl will long remember, somehow epitomizes the welcome and attention to detail which the Trust strives to achieve at its properties.

(Location: Off A96, near Forres, 24 m E of Inverness, Highland.)

Granny's Christmas Pudding

There is a family in Forfar in the County of Angus for whom Christmas would be unthinkable without this pudding on the dinner table, the recipe from several generations of grannies.

450 g (1 lb) kidney suet, chopped finely and minced
450 g (1 lb) white breadcrumbs
125 g (4 oz) plain flour
450 g (1 lb) sultanas
450 g (1 lb) muscatels
450 g (1 lb) blue raisins
125 g (4 oz) mixed peel
125 g (4 oz) glacé cherries (or more)

½ 5 ml spoon (½ teaspoon) salt
450 g (1 lb) dark brown moist sugar
1 5 ml spoon (1 teaspoon) mixed spice
10 eggs, well beaten
1 wine glass rum
1 wine glass brandy

Mix all the dry ingredients thoroughly. Add the liquids and stir vigorously. If the mixture is too dry add a little milk. This quantity boiled in one bowl or floured cloth needs a very large pot in which to boil it. It is therefore probably easier and more convenient to divide it into three equal portions and to boil the puddings for 5–6 hours in individual bowls or in well-floured cloths. The latter way makes a more traditional pudding. This mixture will make 1 large pudding or 4 medium puddings 700–900 g (1½–2 lb).

Mint Sauce

Like lemon balm or 'melissa', mint has a myriad uses. Its aroma in the middle of winter is a reminder that spring will follow.

fresh mint leaves
450 g (1 lb) sugar

600 ml (1 pint) vinegar

REMOVE the leaves from the stalk when the mint is young. Wash well. Chop finely and put in a bowl with enough boiling water poured over the leaves to cover them. Put the sugar into a pan with the vinegar, bring to the boil, simmer for 5 minutes and leave to cool. Strain the water from the mint. Put the mint into jars, nearly filling them. Cover with the cold vinegar liquid. When required for use, take 1 or 2 tablespoons of the mint and make up to 150 ml (¼ pint) with a further mixture of vinegar and water to taste. Always use an enamelled pan when cooking with vinegar, to prevent discolouration.

Pickled Pears

An excellent and different accompaniment to cold meats.

300 ml (½ pint) vinegar
450 g (1 lb) sugar
900 g (2 lb) pears
cloves

1 5 ml spoon (1 teaspoon)
cinnamon or a small piece of
cinnamon stick

PUT the vinegar and sugar into a white-lined pan and cook very slowly for 15 minutes. Skin the pears, stick each with 2 cloves and put them in the syrup. Cook very slowly until soft but not broken. Add the cinnamon. Store in a jar with a screw-top lid.

Raspberry Vinegar

This very old recipe is now to be seen in many health shops. It is an effective drink for colds and flu.

1 kg (2 lb) fresh raspberries
2 litres (4 pints) vinegar

sugar

PICK and clean the raspberries and drain well. Pour the vinegar over them and allow to stand in a covered dish for 4 days, stirring every day. Strain, and add 450 g (1 lb) sugar to every 600 ml (1 pint) of juice. Bring slowly to the boil and simmer for 20 minutes. Bottle when cold and cork tightly for winter use.

Rhubarb Chutney

Do not use the tender pink stalks of new spring rhubarb for this—wait a little until the fruit is more mature.

1 kg (2½ lb) rhubarb
900 g (2 lb) onions
1 litre (2 pints) vinegar
1 5 ml spoon (1 teaspoon) salt
1 5 ml spoon (1 teaspoon) allspice

1 5 ml spoon (1 teaspoon) black pepper
900 g (2 lb) brown sugar
1 5 ml spoon (1 teaspoon) ground cloves

CUT up the rhubarb and put the onions through a mincer or chop very finely and boil in the vinegar in an enamel pan for 20 minutes. Add the other ingredients and boil gently for a further 1 hour. When cool, put into screw-top jars and cover in the usual way.

Inverewe Garden

FAR WEST IN ROSS and Cromarty, in north-west Scotland on the same latitude as Leningrad, lies Inverewe. Here the beneficent effects of the warm currents of the Gulf Stream (or North Atlantic Drift) on the western coast of Scotland allow a profusion of plants from warmer climates to flourish in a generally unlikely latitude.

The whole area is Mackenzie country. Osgood Mackenzie's family had always loved beautiful trees and flowers, and he grew up in an atmosphere of learning and appreciation. In 1862 Osgood Mackenzie bought Inverewe. At that time, and in that poor soil, there was 'only one tiny bush of dwarf willow' to be seen, but with great enthusiasm he set about creating the wonderful property which is really many gardens in one, enjoyed each year by over 100 000 visitors from all over the world.

After purchasing the Inverewe peninsula, Mackenzie's first act was to bring in soil to mix with broken rock to make beds for the plants he wished to grow. He then established windbreaks of pine and fir, bird cherry and larch to provide shelter for the garden he was to spend sixty years making. Now the whole world has come to Inverewe in the form of plants from Chile, China, New Zealand, Burma, California and Nepal. One plant of special interest is a Rhododendron Giganteum from China. It is the largest of all known rhododendrons and grows to eighty feet high in the wild. The seeds of this plant were brought home by George Forrest, one of a company of illustrious Scottish plant collectors.

A continual display of colour throughout the year attracts botanists, professional gardeners and amateurs alike to this Highland garden, for there is a wealth of exotic and interesting plants at Inverewe where people go to enjoy themselves–and to learn.

The Trust restaurant, overlooking the loch, serves a good selection of local Scottish food.

(Location: On A832, 6 m NE of Gairloch, Wester Ross, Highland Region.)

Rowan Jelly

The colour of rowan jelly seems like the distillation of a glorious sunny autumn day when the berries would be gathered.

900 g (2 lb) apples   sugar
900 g (2 lb) rowan berries

CUT up the apples and put them with the rowan berries into a pan and cover with water. Boil for 40 minutes. Strain through a jelly bag. Measure the juice and return to the pan. Allow 450 g (1 lb) sugar to 600 ml (1 pint) of juice. Boil for 30 minutes. Test for set by spooning a little on to a plate (see page 101). Pour into warmed jars and seal at once. This is an excellent accompaniment to grouse, venison or saddle of mutton.

Wild Damson Curd

THERE are two ways of obtaining the flesh of the damson. One way is to bake damsons in the oven for long enough for the skin to crack, when it may be peeled off easily. Another method is to put the damsons into a large pan and stir over a very low heat until soft enough to put through a sieve. Put the pulp into a preserving pan with 350 g (12 oz) of sugar to each 450 g (1 lb) of fruit. If preferred, 450 g (1 lb) of sugar may be added to the fruit if extra sweetness is liked. Stir the sugar well into the pulp and simmer gently for 1 hour, then boil quickly for 20 minutes. Pour into warmed jars and cover. Extra flavour may be added to the damson curd by cracking half the damson stones, blanching the kernels and adding these, tied in muslin, when the cooking is half completed.

Index

111